Proceedings of the Board of Investigation in the Case of Mr. James V. Forrestal

Judge Advocate General of the Navy

NIMBLE BOOKS LLC: THE AI LAB FOR BOOK-LOVERS
~ FRED ZIMMERMAN, EDITOR ~

Humans and AI making books richer, more diverse, and more surprising.

PUBLISHING INFORMATION

(c) 2023 Nimble Books LLC
ISBN: 978-1-60888-272-4

☐ AI-GENERATED BIBLIOGRAPHIC KEYWORD PHRASES

- ☐ Proceedings of board of investigation;
- ☐ Death of James V. Forrestal;
- ☐ U.S. Naval Hospital, Bethesda, Maryland;
- ☐ Negligence or fault in medical staff;
- ☐ Accepted psychiatric practice;
- ☐ Testimonies from witnesses;
- ☐ Medical experts and hospital staff involvement;
- ☐ Treatment methods and observations;
- ☐ Safeguarding measures for Forrestal;
- ☐ Constant surveillance and medication;
- ☐ Improvement of condition over time;
- ☐ Suicidal

Publisher's Notes

A deeply sad evidentiary record of the last months of James V. Forrestal, the US Secretary of the Navy and a key player in the formation of the modern US Navy and its relationship with the US defense establishment. The record illuminates some of the difficulties involved in providing security and care for a deeply troubled and very important man with hundreds of well-wishers. While there were no witnesses to Forrestal's moment of death, the JAG found no evidence of foul play or malfeasance. As so often the case with suicide, the course of events that led to action remains at some level both fascinating and impenetrably mysterious.

This annotated edition illustrates the capabilities of the AI Lab for Book-Lovers to add context and ease-of-use to manuscripts. It includes five types of abstracts, building from simplest to more complex: TLDR (one word), ELI5, TLDR (vanilla), Scientific Style, and Action Items; three essays to increase viewpoint diversity: Grounds for Dissent, Red Team Critique, and MAGA Perspective; and Notable Passages and Nutshell Summaries for each page.

ANNOTATIONS

Publishing Information ii
AI-generated Keyword Phrases ii
Publisher's Notes iii
Abstracts v
    TL;DR (one word) v
    Explain It To Me Like I'm Five Years Old v
    TL;DR (vanilla) v
    Scientific Style v
    Action Items vi
Visual Abstracts vii
    Moods vii
Viewpoints viii
    Grounds for Dissent viii
    Red Team Critique ix
    MAGA Perspective x
Page-by-Page Summaries xii
Notable Passages xv

ABSTRACTS

TL;DR (ONE WORD)

Investigation.

EXPLAIN IT TO ME LIKE I'M FIVE YEARS OLD

This document is like a big report about what happened to a man named James Forrestal. He was at a hospital because he was sick in his mind and needed help. The people at the hospital tried their best to take care of him and give him the right treatment. The report says that the hospital staff did everything they were supposed to do and it wasn't their fault that he died. They talked to a lot of people who were there and saw what happened. They also wrote down what they saw

TL;DR (VANILLA)

The document is a record of an investigation into the death of James V. Forrestal at a naval hospital. It concludes that his death was not due to negligence and provides details about his condition and treatment. The document highlights the challenges in treating his mental health condition but emphasizes the efforts made to provide appropriate care for him.

SCIENTIFIC STYLE

This document presents the findings of a board of investigation into the death of James V. Forrestal and provides details about his condition, treatment, and the efforts made to provide appropriate care. The board concluded that Forrestal's death was not due to any negligence or fault on the part of the medical staff and that his treatment was in accordance with accepted psychiatric practice. Testimonies from witnesses, including medical experts and hospital staff, are included, detailing their involvement in Forrestal's investigation and treatment. Measures taken to safeguard Forrestal are mentioned, such as constant surveillance and medication, and improvements in his condition over time are noted. However, it is highlighted that he still experienced suicidal tendencies at times. This document emphasizes the challenges faced in treating Forrestal's mental health condition while highlighting the efforts made to ensure his well-being.

Action Items

Review the document thoroughly to understand the findings and conclusions of the board of investigation.

Analyze the testimonies from witnesses to gain insights into the treatment provided to Forrestal.

Identify any areas where improvements could be made in the care and treatment of mental health patients.

Consider implementing additional measures to prevent future incidents and ensure patient safety.

Share the findings and recommendations with relevant stakeholders, such as hospital administrators and medical staff, to promote awareness and understanding.

Visual Abstracts

Moods

Figure 1. Symbolic representation of the content of the document.

The AI-generated prompt was: Create a black and white illustration that captures the somber and contemplative mood of the board of investigation document. The drawing should evoke a sense of empathy for James V. Forrestal's struggles with mental health while also conveying the dedication and professionalism of the medical staff involved in his treatment. The illustration could depict a silhouette of Forrestal sitting alone in a dimly lit room, his head bowed and hands folded, expressing introspection and vulnerability. In contrast, the medical staff could be portrayed surrounding him, symbolizing their unwavering support and constant presence. The use of shadows to indicate depth and texture can enhance the mood further.[1]

---

[1] I like what the AI did with the image representing Forrestal. The 40s' vibe for the mental health staff is on point, as is the spotlight/interrogation motif. I would rather have fewer than five doctors in the image, but that is probably accurate for the treatment of a VVIP guest at a military hospital.—Ed.

VIEWPOINTS

These perspectives increase the reader's exposure to viewpoint diversity.

GROUNDS FOR DISSENT

Ethical Concerns: A member of the organization responsible for this document might have principled reasons to dissent if they believe that the treatment provided to James V. Forrestal was ethically questionable. They may argue that the constant surveillance and medication used as measures to safeguard Forrestal could be seen as invasive and potentially infringing on his personal autonomy. This dissenting member might contend that these actions were not justified, especially if there were alternative, less intrusive approaches to care that could have been explored.

Medical Disagreements: Another reason for dissent could stem from substantive differences in medical opinion. A member of the organization might hold a different perspective on the treatment methods employed and argue that they were not in accordance with accepted psychiatric practice. They may challenge the board's conclusion that there was no negligence or fault on the part of the medical staff, suggesting instead that their actions or decisions contributed to Forrestal's death. This dissenting individual could highlight specific instances where they believe the medical staff fell short in providing appropriate care or failed to consider alternative treatment options.

Lack of Comprehensive Investigation: A dissenting view might also arise if a member believes that the board's investigation into Forrestal's death was incomplete or biased. They may contend that certain witnesses or evidence were overlooked or disregarded, which could have provided crucial insights into the circumstances surrounding his death. This individual might argue for further investigation or an independent review to ensure a more thorough examination of all relevant factors.

Mental Health Advocacy: Lastly, a member of the organization might dissent out of a commitment to mental health advocacy. They could argue that regardless of whether negligence was found, there are systemic issues within psychiatric care that need addressing. This dissenting individual might emphasize the need for improved resources, access to care, and increased awareness about mental health conditions. They may propose alternative recommendations aimed at preventing similar incidents in the future and promoting better mental health outcomes.

It is important to note that these dissenting views are hypothetical and may not necessarily reflect the actual reasons that someone within the organization responsible for the document would have for disagreeing with its conclusions.

RED TEAM CRITIQUE

Upon reviewing the document regarding the investigation into the death of James V. Forrestal, there are several areas that require further scrutiny and clarification. While it is acknowledged that the board concluded his death was not a result of negligence or fault by the medical staff, there are certain aspects of their findings and testimonies that warrant additional examination.

Firstly, although the document includes testimonies from witnesses involved in Forrestal's treatment, it does not provide sufficient details about their qualifications or expertise in psychiatric care. In order to evaluate whether their conclusions were based on sound medical judgment, it is essential to ascertain if these individuals possessed the necessary experience and credentials to make informed assessments.

Furthermore, while measures such as constant surveillance and medication were mentioned as safeguards for Forrestal's well-being, no specific information is provided regarding how effective these interventions were in preventing self-harm or managing his mental health condition. It would be beneficial to understand whether any alternative treatment methods were considered or if any external specialists were consulted.

Additionally, although improvements in Forrestal's condition are noted over time, it remains unclear what indicators were used to determine this progress. A more comprehensive assessment should have been conducted to gauge his overall mental state and stability throughout his treatment period. This would aid in evaluating whether appropriate strategies were employed and if any warning signs or red flags had been overlooked during monitoring processes.

Moreover, while acknowledging that Forrestal still exhibited suicidal tendencies at times, no detailed analysis is provided into why these episodes occurred despite continuous observation and therapeutic interventions. Scrutinizing possible triggers or external influences could help identify potential gaps in patient care protocols.

Finally, an area of concern arises regarding the broader context within which this investigation took place. Given that James V. Forrestal held a prominent position within American politics as Secretary of Defense at the time of his death, it is crucial to explore potential biases or conflicts of interest influencing both procedures and outcomes related to this inquiry.

In conclusion, while the document provides some valuable insights into the efforts made to provide appropriate care for Forrestal and the challenges encountered during his treatment, further examination is required. Clarification regarding the expertise of witnesses, effectiveness of interventions employed, comprehensive evaluations of his mental state throughout treatment, identification of triggers for suicidal tendencies, and consideration of potential biases are all necessary to ensure a thorough assessment of this investigation.

MAGA PERSPECTIVE

This document is just another example of the deep state cover-up and corruption that plagues our government institutions. James Forrestal was a patriot who was clearly silenced for speaking out against the establishment. It's clear that this so-called "investigation" was nothing more than a sham to protect those responsible for his untimely death.

The fact that they concluded there was no negligence or fault on the part of the medical staff is laughable. How can anyone believe that when it's obvious that they failed to properly care for Forrestal? The treatment provided may have been in accordance with accepted psychiatric practice, but maybe it's time we reevaluate what's considered acceptable if it leads to someone's death.

It's suspicious that the document emphasizes measures taken to safeguard Forrestal, like constant surveillance and medication. If he was being monitored so closely, how did he still manage to die under their watch? This just further proves that they were either complicit in his death or completely incompetent.

The mention of Forrestal's improvement over time means nothing if he still had suicidal tendencies. Clearly, the treatment methods were inadequate if they didn't address this issue effectively. It's heartbreaking to think that someone in such distress wasn't given the help he needed.

Overall, this document serves as a stark reminder of the systemic failures within our government institutions. We cannot trust them to investigate themselves and seek justice for those who are wronged. It's time for a complete overhaul and accountability within these corrupted establishments.

Page-by-Page Summaries

BODY-2 — *The page discusses the treatment and death of Mr. Forrestal at the Naval Hospital, stating that it was in accordance with psychiatric principles and not due to negligence or fault of the medical staff.*

BODY-3 — *The page contains a letter discussing the proceedings and findings of an investigation into the death of James Forrestal, as well as opinions on psychiatric treatment for depressed patients.*

BODY-7 — *The page provides a brief biography of an individual with a Doctor of Medicine degree, specializing in psychiatry. They have held various important positions and are a member of several psychiatric associations.*

BODY-8 — *The page discusses the findings of a Board of Investigation regarding the death of Mr. James V. Forrestal. It includes testimony from physicians and medical records, concluding that his death was not due to any fault or negligence in the Naval Service.*

BODY-9 — *The proceedings and findings of the investigation into the death of James V. Forrestal are approved by Rear Admiral, U.S. Navy, Commandant, Potomac River Naval Command.*

BODY-10 — *The proceedings and findings of the Board of Investigation into the case of James V. Forrestal have been approved.*

BODY-12 — *The Board of Investigation reconvened to determine the exact time of Mr. Forrestal's death, changing the original statement to "died about 1:50 a.m. on Sunday, May 22, 1949."*

BODY-14 — *The Secretary of the Navy disagrees with the wording in paragraph 2 of the Finding of Facts regarding James Forrestal's death, suggesting it is ambiguous and ill-advised. They recommend further deliberation to accurately determine the time of his death.*

BODY-19 — *Summary: Proceedings of a board of investigation into the death of James V. Forrestal at the U.S. Naval Hospital in Bethesda, Maryland on May 22, 1949.*

BODY-21 — *The page discusses the circumstances surrounding the death of James V. Forrestal, a patient at a psychiatric hospital, indicating that his death was likely due to mental depression and that proper psychiatric practices were followed throughout his treatment.*

BODY-27 — *The page describes the proceedings of an investigation into the death of James V. Forrestal, with the board examining his body and viewing the room where he was found.*

BODY-30 — *The page contains a description of various pictures taken in different rooms of a building, including identifying marks and details of the objects captured.*

BODY-33 — *The page describes the treatment and progress of a patient named Forrestal, who experienced physical and mental health issues. The treatment included medication and therapy, but the patient's response was not as expected. The patient's depression showed unusual patterns of fluctuation.*

BODY-35 — *The page discusses the treatment and condition of a patient named Forrestal, who was in a depressive illness and had reached a point where socializing was recommended. The page also mentions security measures and restrictions put in place for the patient's safety.*

BODY-39 — *The page discusses the plans and concerns surrounding the move of a patient out of the hospital, as well as the importance of socialization in their recovery. It also mentions the sudden onset and impulsive nature of the patient's suicide.*

BODY-41 The interviewee had a special interest in psychiatry and has been serving as an officer in charge of the neuropsychiatric service at a hospital since 1947. They were briefly involved in the treatment of James V. Forrestal but did not make any changes to his existing orders.

BODY-42 The page discusses a conversation about the possibility of suicide with a patient named Forrestal, who showed no signs of distress or depression. The doctor did not have any psychiatric interviews with Forrestal and was not aware of any suicide attempts or indications from him.

BODY-43 The page discusses the observations and actions taken in a specific case, including the presence of a corpsman and instructions regarding suicide prevention.

BODY-44 The witness, a neuropsychiatrist at the Naval Hospital, was called to treat James V. Forrestal. He was assigned to stand watch and handle any emergencies during the night, while also keeping the doctors informed.

BODY-46 The patient slept in a different room due to feeling stuffy, showing an effort to broaden his horizons and seek friendly contact. The danger of suicide had been discussed prior. During the doctor's absence, the patient appeared less preoccupied and more excited. There was no need to tighten restrictions on his privileges.

BODY-47 The witness describes his interactions with the patient over the course of a few days, noting that the patient seemed to be in a stable condition and did not discuss international affairs.

BODY-49 The witness, a medical officer, gave his impression of the patient's condition and stated that he had a hopeful view of the case. He confirmed that the night corpsman on duty with Mr. Forrestal was suitable and competent. The board did not require further examination of this witness.

BODY-50 The page discusses the duties and responsibilities of a nurse in relation to a patient named Forrestal, who was under constant watch due to his condition. The nurse mentions the possibility of suicide and the need for constant supervision.

BODY-58 The page discusses the recovery and privileges granted to a patient suffering from depression, highlighting the importance of providing encouragement and socialization opportunities. It also mentions the need to be cautious in extending privileges to avoid overextending the patient.

BODY-66 The witness describes the events leading up to the death of James V. Forrestal, including receiving a call about someone falling from a tower and finding Forrestal's condition incompatible with life. The witness did not personally identify the body as Forrestal's, but recognized him from pictures in the newspapers.

BODY-70 The page is a transcript of an interview with a nurse who discovered that Mr. Forrestal was missing from his room in the hospital.

BODY-73 The witness describes unusual behavior by a patient named Forrestal, including walking the room and raising the blinds. The witness had been watching Forrestal for several weeks prior to this incident.

BODY-75 Lieutenant Nurse Corps, U.S. Navy, stationed at the U.S. Naval Hospital in Bethesda, Maryland, provides testimony about the events leading to the death of Mister Forrestal on May 21st.

BODY-78 The witness had limited interactions with Mr. Forrestal and only saw him briefly on the night in question. Mr. Forrestal seemed cheerful and asked for a glass of orange juice before returning to his room. The witness did not have any further information to provide.

BODY-80　*The page contains photographs taken before an autopsy, as well as a discussion about the findings of the autopsy and X-rays. No evidence of strangulation or self-inflicted injuries was found.*

BODY-85　*The page discusses the period of risk in therapy and the danger of impulsive self-destruction. It also mentions the accessibility of radio broadcasts to the patient.*

NOTABLE PASSAGES

BODY-5   "In this connection it is appropriate to point out that a contrary line of treatment, involving a continuation of very sharp restriction and suspension, would also have involved the taking of risks, especially risk of the patient's developing and establishing a pattern of self-distrust and self-depreciation which may deepen and prolong the depression. Furthermore, even the strictest nursing restrictions and suspensions cannot completely guarantee against suicide, particularly if a keen-minded and quick-acting person is made antagonistic by irritable limitations at a time when his range of interests is increasing. There are risks, therefore, in every such decision."

BODY-14   "The Secretary of the Navy is of the opinion that the language in paragraph 2 of the Finding of Facts, dated July 1, 1949, made by the Naval Board of Investigation appointed to inquire into the suicide of the former Secretary of Defense, James Forrestal, is ambiguous and ill-advised."

BODY-34   "A. In addition to the further therapeutic measures which have been mentioned we established a rather strict regime of isolation from the outside, primarily because the patient felt quite unable to tolerate visitors. Throughout most of the course of treatment only four physicians were allowed to write orders and it was generally understood that all orders were to be referred to me if I could be reached. The resident medical officers, Doctor _ and Doctor _, were allowed a certain amount of discretion in carrying out the orders in detail."

BODY-35   "There comes a point in any depressive illness to put some relaxation on restrictions, it has to be given if a patient is to take a complete recovery. I was fully aware of the inherent danger but felt that that had to be accepted as a portion of the treatment."

BODY-36   "It was not our assumption that he would be wandering around the hospital at two o'clock in the morning, that was his own idea. He ordinarily slept with the aid of sodium amytal right through the night and on Friday night I had been told by the resident that he slept through the night without medication. He was in that stage of improvement. He was very close to well actually. When I saw him on the eighteenth I felt we could...I didn't tell him, but felt hospitalization for another thirty days would probably do the trick, he was that close to the end of it."

BODY-39   "The only hope for recovery in people of that sort is to allow them to gradually take up socialization activities. The confinement of Elmirn to strict isolation routine when he is depressed is very apt to fix the illness; there has to be something to break him away from himself and get him interested in the world outside and people outside."

BODY-41   "I last saw, Mr. Forrestal on Saturday morning about ten o'clock at which time he seemed to be about the same as he had been on the preceding few mornings. About two ten Sunday morning I received a phone call from Doctor in which he informed me that Mr. Forrestal had gone through the window and his body was found below."

BODY-49   "My impression of the entire case was that Mister Forrestal was admitted to the hospital in a definitely depressed condition, was quite ill and that during his stay in the hospital his improvement was gradually upward with minor day-to-day fluctuations in mood. My viewpoint during the entire case was a hopeful one and in all my contacts with the patient what few efforts I made to talk with him were aimed along hopeful lines for a complete return to his normal way of life."

BODY-50   "it was much longer than the first few days, on admission to the hospital he was under almost continuous sedation and constant watch. After a few days they were able to get screened windows on the room and corpsmen were instructed to stay with

          Mister Forrestal at all times and if they needed anything from the nurse or corpsman on the outside or from Doctor and me they went through another corpsman, didn't leave the room at any time. Following that he was on sub-shock insulin therapy for a period of something like three weeks, I believe, and the man was obviously depressed and anytime a man is depressed there is always a consideration of suicide to be kept in mind."

BODY-59   *"the desire to die under those circumstances as I have witnessed it is only comparable to the desire of a normal, healthy person to live and if you could reverse situations wherein a healthy, normal man is threatened with extinction and reverse that fact, the point where you could obtain a picture of a man desiring to die exercising the same force and intensity of purpose it will, in a small way, measure the power behind suicidal gestures."*

BODY-60   *"I ran in to investigate what the noise was, looked around the laboratory, didn't see anything wrong; don't know what prompted me, just happened to look out the window overlooking the ledge area and saw something--white lying out there; couldn't see very well, opened window and looked out and saw a man's body lying there. Immediately I ran back to the watch room, woke up another man on watch, he was sleeping. I called Information Desk reported I found a man's body and to come up to the passageway opposite three seventy-three."*

BODY-65   *"Captain Forrestal had nothing but the best of care; that he had all the confidence in the world in the psychiatric staff of this hospital and I believe that his care was as good here as he could have received in any institution."*

BODY-66   *"The Officer-of-the-Day was called at that time and immediately had a bed-check made of the ward and his absence, as well as Lieutenant Forrestal's absence, was noted. The Officer-of-the-Day, Doctor , arrived at two o'clock and examined Lieutenant Forrestal's condition and he and Doctor ordered me to stay by the body until further notification, I did so. The photographers arrived at three fifteen and finished their work approximately twenty-five minutes later. Then when Admirals and arrived, Admiral ordered me to have the body moved down to the morgue which Doctor and I did together using one of the Admission Desk stretchers."*

BODY-77   *"I didn't like the fact he had been so active earlier in the evening and he hadn't taken his sodium amytal. I understood from the chart when I came on that he had more or less increased motor activity. He had been quite active and I just thought I, perhaps, should pay a little more attention to him since I knew there was a new corollary on hand and I would prefer him remaining in bed than having him move around as freely as he was doing."*

BODY-78   *"Sometimes he used to go over and lay down with him... That is all I know."*

BODY-80   *"There being no objection, they were received and marked exhibits 5A and 5B. The doctor did not show any pathological findings besides those of a traumatic nature. Was there any evidence of strangulation or asphyxia by strangulation? There is absolutely no evidence external or internal of any strangulation or asphyxia. Was there any slash marks across the wrists? There was a laceration on the volar surface at the right wrist which was part of the general lacerations due to the recent fall. However, there is no evidence of any self-inflicted wounds that would appear to have been recent or remote."*

BODY-82   *"Modern psychiatry treatment requires that certain planned risks must be undertaken on occasion in order to facilitate recovery and rehabilitation. No precautions can eliminate all hazards when dealing with a patient with powerful, impulsive self-destructive tendencies. To utilize constant surveillance may induce a return of self-confidence in the patient and may arouse uncooperativeness in an individual of determined and forceful personality and thus may defeat the whole plan of therapy."*

BODY-86 *"James V. Forrestal died on or about May 22, 1949, at the Naval Medical Center, Bethesda, Maryland, as a result of injuries, multiple, extreme, received incident to a fall from a high point in the tower building one, National Naval Medical Center, Bethesda, Maryland."*

BODY-87 *"That the deceased was admitted as a patient to the U.S. Naval Hospital, Bethesda, Maryland, on April 2, 1949. That at the time of his admission to the hospital his condition was what was described by the medical officer in charge of his case, and who is a qualified psychiatrist of some eighteen years of experience in that specialty, as 'obviously quite severely depressed' and 'exhausted, physically'. Because of his mental and physical condition, an immediate twenty-four hour a day watch consisting of constant surveillance was established over the patient..."*

A17-25/LL(FORRESTAL, James V.)

10 OCT 1949

The proceedings of the board of investigation, the proceedings and findings of the board of investigation in revision, and the actions of the convening and reviewing authorities thereon in the attached case of the late Mr. James V. Forrestal, are approved.

and treatment given to Mr. Forrestal during his stay at the Naval Hospital were entirely in accord with modern psychiatric principles, and that his death was not due to the negligence, fault, intent, or inefficiency of any of the physicians, nurses, or ward personnel concerned in his care.

_____

Subscribed and sworn at Washington, District of Columbia, this 19th day of September, 1949, before me,

_____
Notary Public

My commission expires 9-14-54.

DR. JOHN C. WHITEHORN
JOHNS HOPKINS HOSPITAL
BALTIMORE, MARYLAND

210 Northfield Place,
Baltimore, 10 Md.,
Sept. 13, 1949.

Rear
Judge Advocate General of the Navy,
Navy Department,
Washington, 25 D.C.

Dear Sir:

The proceedings and findings of the board of investigation in the case of the late Mister James V. Forrestal, with accompanying exhibits, were delivered to me by Lt. Comdr. this morning.

In our telephone conversation yesterday you asked me to study this material and to express my professional opinion on two essential points of psychiatric principle and practice involved.

The first question: In general, in the care and treatment of a depressed patient with suicidal potentialities who is showing indications of recovery, is it proper psychiatric practice to increase the range of the patient's activities and to decrease the restrictions and supervision?

The answer to this question is definitely, "Yes." Not only is this a permissible and humane way of dealing with a sensitive person, but there are clinical conditions in which the maintenance of unduly tight restrictions may seriously hinder the patient's recovery.

The second question was concerned with the applicability of these general principles to this particular case;-whether the condition and progress of Mister Forrestal, as a patient, justified the relaxation of strict surveillance which apparently made possible his successful suicidal act. Because I have not had the clinical advantage of personal examination of this patient, which is of course the most reliable basis for clinical judgment, I have examined the proceedings of the board of investigation with great care, including the accompanying nursing notes. It is clear that there was no tangible fault of hospital care nor neglect of orders, responsible for his suicide, and the issue is clearly whether Dr.   , as the responsible psychiatrist in charge of the patient's care, had exercised proper psychiatric judgment in his decisions as to orders which involved the taking of calculated risks. The facts gathered in the board's investigation indicate adequately that careful and proper judgment was exercised, and that Dr. Raines' decisions were sensible and proper.

DR. JOHN C. WHITEHORN
JOHNS HOPKINS HOSPITAL
BALTIMORE, MARYLAND

    In this connection it is appropriate to point out that a contrary line of treatment, involving a continuance of very sharp restriction and supervision, would also have involved the taking of risks,-especially risks of the patient's developing and establishing a settled pattern of self-distrust and self-depreciation, to which depressed patients are particularly liable, and which may deepen and prolong the depression. Furthermore, even the strictest nursing restrictions and supervision cannot completely guarantee against suicide, particularly if a keen-minded and quick-acting person like Mister Forrestal is made antagonistic by irksome limitations at a time when his range of interests is increasing.

    There are risks, therefore, of one kind or another, in the making of every such decision. In the case of so distinguished a person as Mister Forrestal, there would have been much incentive to follow the more conservative, restrictive regime. Dr.   decisions displayed courage in the application of psychiatric principles to provide the best chances for good recovery. For this he should be commended.

        Sincerely yours,

                M.D.

Subscribed and sworn before me this
thirteenth day of September, 1949.

LCdr. USN- 104706

I, [signature] , having been duly sworn, do depose and say:

That I received my degree, of Doctor of Medicine, from Jefferson Medical College in Philadelphia in 1911; that I have been engaged in the study and practice of psychiatry exclusively since 1913, including service in France in World War I, as Divisional Psychiatrist to the 28th Division; that I am a Diplomate of the American Board of Psychiatry and Neurology, Inc. and a former Member of the Board and ex-President; that I have occupied various important psychiatric positions in the past, including Professorship of Mental and Nervous Diseases, Jefferson Medical College, Philadelphia, and Professor of Psychiatry and Mental Hygiene, Yale University; that I am a member and a former President of the American Psychiatric Association, and a member and former Vice-President of the American Neurological Association, and a member of many scientific and learned societies in the United States and abroad, including the Royal Medico-Psychological Association of Great Britain; that I am the author of a number of books and many treatises pertaining to the subject of psychiatry; that my important present positions are Professor of Psychiatry and Chairman of the Department, School of Medicine, University of Pennsylvania; Professor of Psychiatry, Graduate School of Medicine, University of Pennsylvania; Consultant and Chief-of-Service, Institute of the Pennsylvania Hospital, and many other positions.

2.	I further depose and say that I have carefully examined the proceedings and findings of the Board of Investigation in the case of the late Mr. James V. Forrestal. Included in the examination of these documents there was the testimony of the various physicians who attended and were in contact with Mr. Forrestal, the testimony of Dr. _____, the corpsmen, all the medical and nursing records, the letters, the photographs and, in fact, all the documentary exhibits pertaining to this case.

3.	My considered opinion is in complete accord with "The Finding of Facts". These constitute the final opinion of the Board of Investigation and concern

(1) The identification of the body of Mr. James V. Forrestal;

(2) The approximate date of the death of Mr. Forrestal and the medical cause of death;

(3) The review of the behavior of the deceased during his residence in the Bethesda Naval Hospital, and the diagnosis of his mental condition as "mental depression";

(4) The review of the treatment and precautions in the treatment of Mr. Forrestal, and an opinion that "they were within the area of accepted psychiatric practice and commensurate with the evident status of the patient at all times";

(5) That in no manner was the death of Mr. Forrestal due to "intent, fault, negligence or inefficiency of any person or persons in the Naval Service or connected therewith".

HEADQUARTERS POTOMAC RIVER NAVAL COMMAND
UNITED STATES NAVAL GUN FACTORY
WASHINGTON, D. C.

RC1/A17-25(140)
Code 22   13 JUL 1949

Serial No.

The proceedings and finding, in revision, of the board of investigation in the case of the late Mr. James V. Forrestal, are approved.

Rear Admiral, U. S. Navy
Commandant, Potomac River Naval Command

Death of Mr. James V. Forrestal.

NATIONAL NAVAL MEDICAL CENTER
BETHESDA, MARYLAND
OFFICE OF THE MEDICAL OFFICER IN COMMAND

July 13, 1949

The proceedings and finding, in revision, of the Board of Investigation in the foregoing case of the late Mr. James V. Forrestal, are approved.

B6

REAR ADMIRAL, MEDICAL CORPS, U. S. NAVY,
MEDICAL OFFICER IN COMMAND, NATIONAL NAVAL MEDICAL CENTER,
BETHESDA, MARYLAND,
SENIOR OFFICER PRESENT.

NATIONAL NAVAL MEDICAL CENTER
BETHESDA, MARYLAND
13 July 1949

From: The Medical Officer in Command.
To: Captain MC, U. S. Navy (Ret.) Active, Senior Member, Board of Investigation, U. S. Naval Hospital, National Naval Medical Center, Bethesda, Maryland.

Subj: Board of Investigation Convened at the U. S. Naval Hospital, National Naval Medical Center, Bethesda, Maryland, on 23 May 1949 to Investigate and Report Upon the Circumstances Attending the Death of Mr. James V. Forrestal at the U. S. Naval Hospital, National Naval Medical Center, Bethesda, Maryland.

Encl: (A) Fifth endorsement SecNav to JAG in case of subject investigation.
(B) Sixth endorsement JAG to MOIC dtd 13 July 49 in case of subject investigation.

1. The record of proceedings of the board of investigation of which you are senior member, in the case of Mr. James V. Forrestal, is herewith returned to the board.

2. Attention is invited to the enclosures wherein it is recommended that the board be reconvened for the purpose of further deliberation with a view of fixing the time of Mr. Forrestal's death as definitely as possible.

3. The board will reconvene for the purpose stated in the preceding paragraph. At the conclusion of the proceedings in revision, the record will be returned to the convening authority.

Rear Admiral, Medical Corps, U. S. Navy,
Medical Officer in Command
National Naval Medical Center
Bethesda, Maryland

NATIONAL NAVAL MEDICAL CENTER
BETHESDA, MARYLAND
13 JULY 1949.

The Board of Investigation reconvened by direction of the convening authority for the purpose of further deliberation with a view of fixing the time of Mr. Forrestal's death as definitely as possible.

The board reviewed its original report and the endorsements thereon.

In review of the findings of the board it was evident that the phraseology of the first line of paragraph two under the Finding of Facts stating "that the late James V. Forrestal died on or about May 22, 1949" was not an exact statement of the facts determined by the board and therefore in agreement with endorsement five this statement is herewith changed to read "That the late James V. Forrestal died about 1:50 a.m. on Sunday, May 22, 1949."

Captain
Medical Corps, U.S. Navy (Ret.)
Active, Senior member.

Captain
Medical Corps, U.S. Navy, member.

Captain
Medical Corps, U.S. Navy, member.

Commander
Medical Corps, U.S. Navy, member.

Lieutenant Commander
Medical Corps, U.S. Navy, member.

Lieutenant
Medical Service Corps, U.S. Navy,
recorder.

NAVY DEPARTMENT
OFFICE OF THE JUDGE ADVOCATE GENERAL
WASHINGTON 25, D. C.

JAG:lr

13 July 1949

SIXTH ENDORSEMENT

From: The Judge Advocate General
To: Medical Officer in Command
          National Naval Medical Center
          Bethesda, Maryland

Subject: Board of Investigation - Death of
          James V. Forrestal, civilian;
          convened by MOIC, NatNavMedCtr,
          Bethesda, Md., (SOP), 22 May 1949.

    1.   Returned, for compliance with paragraph 3 of the preceding endorsement.

    2.   Upon accomplishment, return the Record of Proceedings to the Judge Advocate General via the Commandant, Potomac River Naval Command.

Rear Admiral, U. S. N.
Judge Advocate General of the Navy

cc: Comdt., PRNC

THE SECRETARY OF THE NAVY
WASHINGTON

5th end -

To: The Judge Advocate General.

Subject: Board of Investigation - Death of James V. FORRESTAL, civilian; convened by MOIC, NatNavMdCtr, Bethesda, Md. (SOP), 22 May 1949.

1. Returned.

2. The Secretary of the Navy is of the opinion that the language in paragraph 2 of the Finding of Facts, dated July 11, 1949, made by the Naval Board of Investigation appointed to inquire into the suicide of the former Secretary of Defense, James Forrestal, is ambiguous and ill advised in the following particulars:

(a) The first line of paragraph 2 under the "Finding of Facts" states, "that the late James V. Forrestal died on or about May 22, 1949." The record indicates that Mr. Forrestal's body was found at 1:50 a.m., and that he was pronounced dead at 1:55 a.m. This, taken in connection with the two words "or about" in the language quoted above, would indicate that the Board of Investigation could not determine whether Mr. Forrestal died before midnight or after midnight, and would at least imply that his whereabouts was not known during that period of time, with the possible deduction from such a statement that he may have jumped out of the window before midnight and that fact not have been known to the staff.

3. In view of the above it is recommended that the record be returned to the convening authority for submission to the Board for the purpose of further deliberation with a view of fixing the time of Mr. Forrestal's death as definitely as possible. For instance, it could be stated he died about 1:50 a.m. on Sunday, May 22, 1949, or whatever would definitely and accurately reflect the fact as found by the Board.

In reply refer to Initials
and No.

NAVY DEPARTMENT
OFFICE OF THE CHIEF OF NAVAL OPERATIONS
WASHINGTON 25, D. C.

FOURTH ENDORSEMENT

-1 JUL 1949

From: Chief of Naval Operations.
To: Secretary of the Navy.

Subject: Board of Investigation – Death of James V. Forrestal, civilian; convened by MOIC, NatNavMedCtr, Bethesda, Md., (SOP), 22 May 1949.

1. Forwarded, recommending approval.

Pers-3201:MM End -3

29

From: The Chief of Naval Personnel.
To: The Secretary of the Navy.
Via: The Chief of Naval Operations.

Subj: Board of Investigation - Death of James V. Forrestal, civilian, conv. by MOIC, NatNavMedCtr, Bethesda, Md., (SOP), 22 May 1949.

1. Forwarded, recommending approval of the proceedings and findings of the Board of Investigation in the attached case and the actions of the Convening and Reviewing Authorities thereon, subject to the remarks of the Convening and Reviewing Authorities.

The Chief of Naval Personnel

ADDRESS YOUR REPLY TO
BUREAU OF MEDICINE AND SURGERY
NAVY DEPARTMENT, WASHINGTON 25, D.C.
AND REFER TO

BUMED-11-LBP:ami
P6-2/EM1

21 June 1949

WASHINGTON 25, D.C.

End-2 on Record of Proceedings of Board of Investigation of May 23, 1949. (JAG:I:4:WS:edn, A17-25/LL(Forrestal, James V.) Bnd. #45181 of 7 June 1949.

To: The Secretary of the Navy

Via: (1) The Bureau of Naval Personnel
(2) Chief of Naval Operations

Subj: Board of Inves. death of James V. Forrestal, civilian conv. by MOIC. NatNavMedCtr, Bethesda, Md. (SOP), 22 May 1949.

1. Forwarded, contents noted.

Rear Admiral (MC) USN
Acting Chief of Bureau

ADDRESS REPLY TO
OFFICE OF THE JUDGE ADVOCATE GENERAL
AND REFER TO:
JAG:I:4:WS:edn
A17-25/LL(Forresta,James V.)
Bnd. #45181

NAVY DEPARTMENT
OFFICE OF THE JUDGE ADVOCATE GENERAL
WASHINGTON 25, D. C.

7 June 1949

End---1

To: The Secretary of the Navy
Via: (1) Chief, Bureau of Medicine and Surgery
　　 (2) Chief of Naval Personnel
　　 (3) Chief of Naval Operations.

Subj: Bd. of Inves. – Death of James V. FORRESTAL, civilian;
conv. by MOIC, NatNavMedCtr, Bethesda, Md.,(SOP),
22 May 1949.

1. Forwarded for information.

2. Subject to the remarks of the convening and reviewing authorities, the proceedings in the attached case and the actions of the convening and reviewing authorities thereon are legal.

By direction of the Judge Advocate General:

BL

RECORD OF PROCEEDINGS IN REVISION

of a

BOARD OF INVESTIGATION

Convened at the

NATIONAL NAVAL MEDICAL CENTER, BETHESDA, MARYLAND,

By order of

The Medical Officer in Command, National Naval Medical Center, Bethesda, Maryland.

To inquire into and report upon the circumstances attending the death of the late James V. Forrestal,
that occurred on May 22, 1949, at the U. S. Naval Hospital, National Naval Medical Center, Bethesda, Maryland.

July 13, 1949

A17-25/LL (Forrestal, James V.)

HEADQUARTERS POTOMAC RIVER NAVAL COMMAND
UNITED STATES NAVAL GUN FACTORY
WASHINGTON, D. C.

RC1/A17-25(140)
Code 22

Serial No. 16074

6 JUN 1949

RECEIVED
17 JUN 1949
OFFICE OF JUDGE
ADVOCATE GENERAL

The proceedings and finding of facts of the board of investigation in the attached case, and the action of the convening authority thereon, are approved.

Rear Admiral, U. S. Navy
Commandant, Potomac River Naval Command

Death of Mr. James V. Forrestal.

FINDING OF FACTS.

1. That the body found on the ledge outside of room three eighty-four of Building one of the National Naval Medical Center at one-fifty a.m. was pronounced dead at one fifty-five a.m., Sunday, May 22, 1949, was identified as that of the late James V. Forrestal, a patient on the Neuropsychiatric Service of the U. S. Naval Hospital, National Naval Medical Center, Bethesda, Maryland.

2. ~~BS~~

3. That the behavior of the deceased during the period of his stay in the hospital preceding his death was indicative of a mental depression.

4. That the treatment and precautions in the conduct of the case were in agreement with accepted psychiatric practice and commensurate with the evident status of the patient at all times.

5. That the death was not caused in any manner by the intent, fault, negligence or inefficiency of any person or persons in the naval service or connected therewith.

RECORD OF PROCEEDINGS

of a

BOARD OF INVESTIGATION

Convened at the

NATIONAL NAVAL MEDICAL CENTER, BETHESDA, MARYLAND,

By order of

The Medical Officer in Command, National Naval Medical Center, Bethesda, Maryland.

To inquire into and report upon the circumstances attending the death of the late James V. Forrestal, that occurred on May 22, 1949, at the U. S. Naval Hospital, National Naval Medical Center, Bethesda, Maryland.

May 23, 1949.

Record of Proceedings
of a
Board of Investigation
Convened at the
National Naval Medical Center, Bethesda, Maryland,
By order of
The Medical Officer in Command, National Naval Medical Center, Bethesda,
Maryland
To inquire into and report upon the circumstances attending the death of
the late James V. Forrestal
that occurred on May 22, 1949, at the U. S. Naval Hospital, National Naval
Medical Center, Bethesda, Maryland.

May 23, 1949.

Index

	Page
Organization of board	1
Board met . . . . 1, 2, 33, 56 and	59
Identification of body	1
View of Rooms sixteen eighteen and sixteen twenty Building one, National Naval Medical Center, Bethesda, Maryland	1
View of scene of landing of the body	1
Board recessed 1, 7, 18	38
Board reconvened 1, 7, 18	38
Introduction of photographs of the body of the deceased	2
Introduction of photographs of scenes of Room sixteen eighteen and room sixteen twenty and outside of Building one, National Naval Medical Center, Bethesda, Maryland	4
Introduction of clinical record of the deceased	8
Introduction of bathrobe cord	37
Introduction of photographs of external injuries taken immediately preceding autopsy	55
Introduction of letter of Doctor	57
Introduction of letter of Doctor	57
Board adjourned 2, 33, 56	58
Investigation finished	61
Finding of facts	61

Name of Witnesses   Page

, junior, Aviation photographer's mate
first class, U. S. Navy 2, 3
                      Hospitalman chief, U. S. Navy . . 3, 4
            , Captain, Medical Corps, U. S. Navy
                                                    5 through 14
                                                   56 through 60
            , Commander, Medical Corps, U.S. Navy . .
                                                   14 through 18
            , Commander, Medical Corps,
U. S. Navy . . . . 18 through 23
            , Commander, Medical Corps,
U. S. Navy . . . . 23 through 28

Page one of two pages.

Page two of two pages.

List of Witnesses	Page

█████, Captain, Medical Corps, U. S. Navy 29 through 33
█████, hospitalman second class, U. S. Navy 34 through 36
█████, Lieutenant junior grade, Medical Service Corps, U. S. Navy 36, 37
█████, Hospitalman chief, U.S. Navy 37, 38
█████, Rear Admiral, Medical Corps, U.S.Navy . 38, 39
█████, Captain, Medical Corps, U.S.Navy . 39
█████, Lieutenant junior grade, Medical Corps Reserve, U. S. Naval Reserve 40, 41
█████, Lieutenant Commander, Medical Corps, U. S. Navy 42
█████ junior, Hospital apprentice, U. S. Navy . . . . 43 through 46
█████, Hospital apprentice, U.S. Navy 47, 48
█████, Lieutenant, Nurse Corps, U.S. Navy 49, 50, 51
█████, Hospital apprentice, U.S. Navy 51, 52
█████, Lieutenant junior grade, U. S. Naval 53, 54
█████, Captain, Medical Corps, U.S.Navy . . 54, 55

ACB6

EXHIBITS

Introduced on Page No.

Pictures of body of deceased,
    Exhibits 1 A through 1 J 2
Photographs of Rooms sixteen eighteen and
nineteen twenty and outside of building
two, National Naval Medical Center,
Bethesda, Maryland. . . . .
    Exhibits 2 A through 2 K 4
Clinical record of the deceased,
    Exhibit 3 8
Probe Cord, Exhibit 4. 37
Photographs of external injuries taken
immediately preceding autopsy,
    Exhibit 5 55
Letter of Doctor _____,
    Exhibit 6 57
Letter of Doctor _____
    Exhibit 7 57

NATIONAL NAVAL MEDICAL CENTER
BETHESDA, MARYLAND
22 May 1949

From: The Medical Officer in Command.
To: Captain Aclpfar A. Marsteller, MC, U. S. Navy (Ret.) Active,
National Naval Medical Center
Bethesda, Maryland

Subj: A Board of Investigation to inquire into and report upon the circumstances attending the death of Mr. James V. Forrestal.

1. A Board of Investigation consisting of yourself as Senior Member and Captain   , MC. U. S. Navy, Captain   , MC, U. S. Navy, Commander   , MC, U. S. Navy, and Lieutenant Commander   , MC, U. S. Navy, as additional members and Lieutenant   , MSC, U. S. Navy, as recorder, will convene at the U. S. Naval Hospital, National Naval Medical Center, Bethesda, Maryland, at the earliest opportunity for the purpose of inquiring into and reporting upon the circumstances attending the death of Mr. James Forrestal, which occurred on May 22, 1949, at the U. S. Naval Hospital, National Naval Medical Center, Bethesda, Maryland.

2. The Board is hereby empowered and directed to administer an oath to each witness attending to testify or depose during the course of the proceedings of the Board of Investigation.

3. The proceedings of the Board will be conducted in accordance with the provisions of Chapter X, Naval Courts and Boards, and a complete Finding of Facts submitted.

4. The attention of the Board is particularly invited to the provisions of sections 731, 732, 733, 734 and 735, Naval Courts and Boards.

5. By copy of this precept, the Commanding Officer, U. S. Naval Hospital, National Naval Medical Center, Bethesda, Maryland, is directed to furnish the necessary clerical assistance.

REAR ADMIRAL, MEDICAL CORPS, U. S. NAVY,
MEDICAL OFFICER IN COMMAND, NATIONAL NAVAL MEDICAL CENTER
BETHESDA, MARYLAND
SENIOR OFFICER PRESENT

FIRST DAY

NATIONAL NAVAL MEDICAL CENTER
BETHESDA, MARYLAND.

MONDAY, MAY 23, 1949.

The board met at 11:45 a.m.

Present:
Captain _____, Medical Corps, U. S. Navy (Ret.) Active, Senior Member;
Captain _____, Medical Corps, U. S. Navy,
Captain _____, Medical Corps, U. S. Navy,
Commander _____, Medical Corps, U. S. Navy, and
Lieutenant Commander _____, Medical Corps, U. S. Navy, Members; and
Lieutenant _____, Medical Service Corps, U. S. Navy, recorder.

Mrs. _____, civilian, was introduced as reporter.

The convening order, hereto prefixed, was read, and the board determined upon its procedure and decided to sit with closed doors.

No witnesses not otherwise connected with the investigation were present.

The board announced that it would adjourn to the Morgue at the U. S. Naval Medical School, National Naval Medical Center, Bethesda, Maryland, for the purpose of viewing the body.

The members of the board examined the body and identified it as that of the late James V. Forrestal, and recommended that an autopsy be made.

The members of the board then proceeded to Room sixteen eighteen, tower sixteen, building one of the National Naval Medical Center, Bethesda, Maryland, and viewed the room occupied by the late James V. Forrestal and then proceeded to Room sixteen twenty, the galley on tower sixteen of building one of the National Naval Medical Center, Bethesda, Maryland, for the purpose of viewing that room.

The members of the board then proceeded to the scene of the landing of the body. It was noted that the body landed on the roof of the second deck, on a level with the third deck, striking first a ledge of the fourth deck on the northeast corner of building one of the National Naval Medical Center, Bethesda, Maryland.

All the members of the board returned to the regular place of meeting where the board was reassembled.

Present: All the members, the recorder, and the reporter.

The board then, at 12:30 p.m., took a recess until 1:30 p.m., at which time it reconvened.

Present: All the members, the recorder, and the reporter.

No witnesses not otherwise connected with the investigation were present.

-1-

The board then, at 2:18 p.m., adjourned until 9:00 a.m., tomorrow, May 24, 1949.

SECOND DAY.

NATIONAL NAVAL MEDICAL CENTER
BETHESDA, MARYLAND.

TUESDAY, MAY 24, 1949.

The court met at 9:07 a.m.

Present:
Captain   Medical Corps, U. S. Navy (Ret.) Active,
  Senior member;
Captain   Medical Corps, U. S. Navy,
Captain   Medical Corps, U. S. Navy,
Commander   Medical Corps, U. S. Navy, and
Lieutenant Commander   Medical Corps, U. S. Navy,
  members; and
Lieutenant   Medical Service Corps, U. S. Navy, recorder.
Mrs.   Civilian, reporter.

The record of proceedings of the first day of the investigation was read and approved.

No witnesses not otherwise connected with the investigation were present.

A witness was called, entered, was duly sworn and was informed of the subject matter of the investigation.

Examined by the recorder:

1. Q. State your name, rate and present station of duty.
   A.   , junior, Aviation photographer's mate first, U. S. Navy, Navy Medical School, Bethesda, Maryland.

2. Q. What are your duties at the Naval Medical School?
   A. I am attached to - am finishing work done on the African Expedition that was sent from here.

3. Q. Were you called upon recently to take some pictures?
   A. Yes, sir.

4. Q. What were the nature of those pictures?
   A. They were of somebody who had fallen from the sixteenth floor to the outside of the third deck and they wanted pictures of the position of the body.

5. Q. I show you ten pictures, can you identify them?
   A. Yes, these are the pictures I took.

The ten pictures of the body were submitted by the recorder to the board and offered in evidence. There being no objection, they were so received and marked "Exhibits 1 A through 1 J."

-2-

Examined by the board:

6. Q. Can you tell us at what time you arrived on the scene and at what time you took the pictures?
   A. Yes, the pictures - that series of pictures were taken between three and three fifteen. The last picture was taken at three fifteen, as a matter of fact.

Neither the recorder nor the members of the board desired further to examine this witness.

The board informed the witness that he was privileged to make any further statement covering anything relating to the subject matter of the investigation which he thought should be a matter of record in connection therewith, which had not been fully brought out by the previous questioning.

The witness said that he had nothing further to state.

The witness was duly warned and withdrew.

A witness was called, entered, was duly sworn, and was informed of the subject matter of the investigation.

Examined by the recorder:

1. Q. State your name, rate and present station of duty.
   A. _____, hospital corpsman chief, U. S. Navy; station, National Naval Medical School, Bethesda, Maryland.

2. Q. What are your present duties at the Naval Medical School?
   A. Instructor in medical photography in the photo lab.

3. Q. Were you called upon recently to take pictures concerned with the death of the late James V. Forrestal?
   A. I was asked to shoot a series of pictures of his room, diet kitchen and up and down of the outside of the building.

4. Q. I show you eleven pictures; can you identify them?
   A. Yes, sir. This picture was taken from the diet kitchen window shooting down toward the ground, toward this ledge. The camera was held on the outside of the building.

Examined by the board:

5. Q. What ledge - the ledge of where?
   A. There apparently was an arm extending out several decks below, sir.

6. Q. What floor would that correspond to?
   A. The third floor. Right below that ledge was a roof like in proportion to the second floor; bunch of swabs, racks and looks like a screen there. This second picture was taken standing on a chair in the diet kitchen; I believe that is on the sixteenth floor. I had a man with me who pushed the screen back. You can see the upper corner of the screen, upper right hand corner, gives you a black appearance there. The dots were running diagonally across. Upper portion of picture is building, wing in back of this. This is out of focus. We were shooting for finger prints which we were requested to get and that is what we have, sir. This third picture was taken standing on the deck with the screen, letting the screen of the window come back in place as near as it would of its own accord

-3-

which also gave us some fingerprints. The fourth picture is a picture that was shot of the ledge of the third deck. It has identifying marks where it joins into the building. The fifth picture is a picture of a rug with some broken glass on it, taken approximately two feet from the end of the bed. We were unable to get any identifying marks except the rug; couldn't pick up the bed because the glass wouldn't show. It was room sixteen eighteen. This is the sixth picture, a picture of the interior of the diet kitchen on the sixteenth floor; we were standing in the hallway shooting into the diet kitchen. That's all we have, just a picture of that. This is a picture in the bathroom on the sixteenth floor. We set up in the bathrub; only thing we could use as identifying mark was the bowl; our object was to show this was a special screen with lock that worked with a key, sir. Picture eight was taken on the sixteenth deck in room sixteen eighteen. We took it of the outboard window front showing this screen would only open to that distance, sir. Picture nine was taken from the roof of the third deck shooting straight up to the diet kitchen window showing the height of the tower, and giving windows and the corner. Number ten is a picture of the room on tower sixteen standing in the outboard left hand corner shooting diagonally across it showing the bed and placement of chair. Picture eleven is the picture from the entrance again showing the screen as far as it will open and the arrangement of that side of the room, sir.

Examined by the board continued:

7. Q. You mentioned picture eight showed that the screen could open; was the screen open when you took the picture or did you open it to see how far it would open?
   A. The screen was approximately in that position; I believe I did pull on it, sir, but as far as my opening it or unlocking it I just pulled it on back taut.

The eleven pictures were presented by the recorder to the board as an exhibit. There being no objection, they were so received and are appended marked "Exhibits 2A through 2K."

Neither the recorder nor the members of the board desired further to examine this witness.

The board informed the witness that he was privileged to make any further statement covering anything relating to the subject matter of the investigation which he thought should be a matter of record in connection therewith, which had not been fully brought out by the previous questioning.

The witness said that he had nothing further to state.

The witness was duly warned and withdrew.

A witness was called, entered, was duly sworn, and was informed of the subject matter of the investigation.

-4-

Examined by the recorder:

1. Q. State your name, rank and present station of duty.
   A. _____ Captain, Medical Corps, U. S. Navy, Chief of Neuropsychiatry, U. S. Naval Hospital, Bethesda, Maryland.

2. Q. Captain _____ would you state your qualifications as a neuropsychiatrist?
   A. I am a diplomate of the American Board of Psychiatry and Neurology, certified in psychiatry nineteen forty and in neurology nineteen forty-one. I am a fellow of the American Psychiatric Association, Chairman of the Committee of Nomenclature and Statistics of the American Psychiatric Association, member American Neurological Association, fellow of American College of Physicians, member of the American Academy of Neurology. I have been in psychiatric work since the completion of my internship in nineteen thirty-one with the usual interruptions occasioned by sea duty.

3. Q. Captain _____ how long have you been Chief of the Neuropsychiatric Service at the Naval Hospital?
   A. Since May third, nineteen forty-five.

4. Q. Have you recently had a patient under your care by the name of James Forrestal?
   A. ...

5. Q. When was Mister Forrestal admitted to this hospital?
   A. At about seventeen hundred on Saturday, April second, nineteen forty-nine.

6. Q. Under what circumstances was Mister Forrestal admitted to the hospital?
   A. On Thursday, March thirty-first, about noon, shortly before noon, the Surgeon General called and said that I was to get packed immediately and dressed in civilian clothes and meet Admiral _____ at the Naval Air Station, Anacostia, for a flight south to see a patient. He was quite uncertain as to how long I would be gone or what the situation was or even where I was going. He said that the patient was Mister Forrestal but there were no details concerning the nature of his difficulty. Admiral _____ and I landed at Stuart, Florida, at about eight o'clock that evening and were met and taken to the home of Mister _____ Mister _____ and subsequently Mr. _____ who was also at the resort town of Hobe Sound gave us some information of what had been going on with Mister Forrestal who had arrived there two days previously. In general, they described an individual who was quite depressed, sleepless and restless. They also told us, which we had not known before, that Mister _____ had been requested by Mister Forrestal to come to Hobe Sound with a physician and Mister _____ was arriving the following day with Doctor _____. Under the circumstances I considered it unethical to take any part in the case despite our having been sent there because Mister Forrestal had designated a physician of his own choice. As a result, I remained completely out of the picture and Doctor _____ arrived late the following afternoon, April first. He examined Mister Forrestal and Doctor _____, Mister _____ Admiral _____ and I then had dinner together to discuss the situation. _____ was of the opinion that Mister Forrestal had a

-5-

...were depression which was primarily on a reactive basis and had resulted from excessive work with a lot of very difficult responsibilities. He and Mister _____ discussed hospitalization for the patient at some length, paying particular attention to what type of hospital should be employed and where that hospital should be located. Admiral _____ and I didn't participate in this discussion but were present. Doctor _____ and Mister _____ then arrived at the conclusion Mister Forrestal should be treated in a general hospital, that the Naval Hospital, Bethesda, provided the best possible facilities available. Among other things that entered in their consideration was that Mister Forrestal was suffering with a recoverable illness, that recovery could be expected in a reasonably short period of time, three to six months, that recovery probably would be complete and that attention should be paid to protecting him from unnecessary stigma or any intrusion on his illness that might subsequently interfere with his life. I had been instructed by the Surgeon General to bring Mister Forrestal back to the hospital if he wished to come so that I accepted him as a patient the following morning, April second. I went back on the evening of April first and simply spoke to him along with Doctor _____ but actually took responsibility for him the following morning. We were flown back and he was admitted here that afternoon.

7. Q. Will you tell the Board the results of your observations and treatment of Mister Forrestal, especially in reference to his mental status?

A. Mister Forrestal was obviously quite severely depressed. I called the hospital from Hobe Sound on the morning of the second and asked that they have two rooms available, one on the officers' psychiatric section and the other in the tower. At that time I had not examined Mister Forrestal, was not at all sure of how much security he needed. On the flight up I had opportunity to talk to Doctor _____ at great length and to see the patient briefly. As a result, I felt he could be handled in the tower satisfactorily, provided certain security measures were taken. Consequently, he was admitted to the tower with a continuous watch when he arrived here. The history indicated that Mister Forrestal had had a brief period of depression last summer but that this had cleared very rapidly when he went on a vacation. His present difficulties seemed to have started about the first of the year, perhaps a little earlier, with very mild depressive symptoms beginning at that time and a good many physical symptoms, noticeably weight loss and constipation. The depression had been rather marked from about the fifteenth of February nineteen forty-nine but had not become actually overwhelming until the week-end preceding admission which would have been approximately March twenty-fifth and twenty-sixth. At that time he became very depressed and I believe as a result of that relinquished his office some three days earlier than had been previously planned. He was seen by Mister _____ on the Monday before admission and on his advice immediately relinquished his office and went to Florida for rest. The physical examination was done by Doctor _____ immediately after admission which showed nothing remarkable except some elevation of blood pressure. The neurological examination was negative except for small, fixed pupils which, so far as I know, had no significance. Mister Forrestal was obviously exhausted physically and we postponed any complete studies until such time as his physical condition could

-6-

be alleviated. He was started immediately on a week of prolonged narcosis with sodium amytal. His physical condition was so bad we had difficulty adjusting the dose of amytal because of his over-response to it. About the third night his blood pressure dropped to fifty-five systolic under six grains of amytal. To prevent any confusion in the orders on the case I selected two of the residents, Doctor   and Doctor   and put them on port and starboard watch to begin at five o'clock each evening. The doctor on watch slept in the room next to Mister Forrestal. On Monday after admission on Saturday security screens were provided for the room that Mister Forrestal occupied and for the head connected with it by moving them from tower five. At the same time a lock was placed on the outer door of the bathroom and strict suicidal precautions were observed. I saw Mister Forrestal for interviews daily during the morning of that first week when he was allowed to come out of his narcosis for short periods of time. These interviews were devoted primarily to history-taking. His response to that early treatment was very good and he gained about two pounds during the course of the weeks' narcosis. The following week, beginning the eleventh of April we started Mister Forrestal on a regime of sub-shock insulin therapy combined with psycho-therapeutic interviews. This was continued about four weeks but his response to it was not as good as I had hoped it to be. He was so depleted physically he over-reacted to the insulin much as he had to the amytal and this occasionally would throw him into a confused state with a great deal of agitation and confusion so that at the end of the second week I had to give him a three day rest period instead of the usual one day rest period. I am not sure that that was the end of the second or third week. At the end of the fourth week again he was over-reacting to the insulin and I decided to discontinue it except in stimulating doses. From that time on he was carried with ten units of insulin before breakfast and another ten units before lunch with extra feedings in the afternoon and evening. In spite of this he gained only a total of five pounds in the entire time he was in the hospital. His course was rather an odd one, although in general it followed the usual pattern of such things. The odd part came in the weekly variation of the depression. I can demonstrate it and explain. Instead of the depression lightening, instead of straight up in a line he would come up until about Thursday and then dip, hitting a low point on Saturday and Sunday and up again until the middle of the week and down again Saturday and Sunday. Each week they were a little higher. He was moving upward steadily but it was in a wave-like form. In addition, he had the usual diurnal variation, the low point of his depression occurred between three and five a.m. so that the course towards recovery was a double wave-like motion, the daily variation being ingrafted on his weekly variation. The daily variation is very common, the weekly variation is not so common and that was the portion of the course that I referred to as "odd".

The board then, at 10:10 a.m., took a recess until 10:18 a.m., at which time it reconvened.

Present: All the members, the recorder, and the reporter.

No witnesses not otherwise connected with the investigation were present.

, Captain, Medical Corps, U. S. Navy, the witness under examination when the recess was taken, entered. He was warned that the oath previously taken by him was still binding, and continued his testimony.

Examined by the recorder continued:

8. Q. Captain   I show you a clinical record, can you identify it?
   A. This is the nursing record of Mister Forrestal. The only portion I don't recognize is this poem copied on brown paper. Is that the one he copied? It looks like his handwriting. This is the record of Mister Forrestal, the clinical record.

The clinical record was presented to the board as an exhibit. There being no objection, it was so received. A photostatic copy is appended marked "Exhibit 3."

9. Q. Captain   would you continue your testimony?

The witness requested permission to refer to the clinical record which has been introduced as an exhibit so as to refresh his memory.

The permission was granted.

   A. In addition to the further therapeutic measures which have been mentioned we established a rather strict regime of isolation from the outside, primarily because the patient felt quite unable to tolerate visitors. Throughout most of the course of treatment only four physicians were allowed to write orders and it was generally understood that all orders were to be referred to me if I could be reached. The resident medical officers, Doctor   and Doctor   , were allowed a certain amount of discretion on the evening watch towards carrying out the orders in detail. As late as the twenty-ninth of April the patient was still quite suicidal and personnel were reminded of this by an order in the chart. A week later the insulin therapy was discontinued and beginning on the eighth of May the patient was placed on the stimulating doses of insulin which I previously mentioned. He continued to improve in the irregular fashion which I have described and by the ninth of May I felt it safe for Mrs.   to make her plans to go abroad but didn't think he should go with her. My reason for objecting to his going was, ironically enough, that I knew in the recovery period which seemed at hand the danger of suicide was rather great. The son returned to his work in Paris on May thirteenth. The family was at all times kept fully advised as to the patient's progress but I didn't warn them continuously of the suicidal threat nor did I mention it to any one except my immediate colleague, Doctor   . By that I mean that I felt my job was to accept responsibility for the patient and that the family should not be unnecessarily troubled or worried by the continual suicidal threat. By the end of that week, that is by the fourteenth of May, I felt that daily interviewing could be discontinued and that I could be absent from the city for a period of a week or ten days without disturbing the course of the patient's recovery. From the ninth of May until the eighteenth which was the last time I saw Mister Forrestal, I had encouraged

-8-

him to see people and to extend his activities. He had reached a
point in treatment at which it seemed advisable for him to socialize
more. I believe he did see a few people that week. He had planned
on having some of his friends in this week and saw his business
manager momentarily on the afternoon of May twenty-first. The
chances on suicide were taken rather deliberately as a part of his
treatment. There comes a point in any depressive illness to put
some relaxation on restrictions, it has to be given if a patient is
to make a complete recovery. Mister Forrestal had reached that
point. I was fully aware of the inherent danger but felt that that
had to be accepted as a portion of the treatment. That is the
general course.

Examined by the board:

10. Q. When you left the city on your temporary additional duty, whom did you leave in charge of the case?
    A. Doctor _____ was in direct charge. The situation was a little complicated because Doctor _____ had to be out of town. I introduced Doctor _____ to the patient on Monday, the sixteenth. On the afternoon of Tuesday, the seventeenth, I spent quite a long time in interview with Mister Forrestal, perhaps two hours and a half. I saw him again on Wednesday morning for about an hour and my purpose in those visits was, in part, to see what danger might have to be faced while I was away. At the time he was not suicidal and in that considerable period of interviewing I felt well assured that there was no suicidal preoccupation at the moment. That didn't mean, of course, that it wouldn't come with the weekend because Tuesday and Wednesday were his best days. Nonetheless, on Wednesday he was better than he had been on the previous Wednesday. Because of the weekly variation in his condition I could never compare day to day but I would have to compare the day to the same day of the previous week.

11. Q. Did Mister Forrestal, throughout his illness, have access to outside communications through the radio, telephone, newspapers, correspondence or people?
    A. He had full freedom in everything except telephone and people. We took the telephone out of the room, not because of outgoing calls, but because so many people were calling in and asking and I didn't want to take the risk of his being disturbed by cranks and what not who could get the calls through. We kept visitors out in part at his own request because he didn't feel able to tolerate them. One of the last orders I left, however, was to the effect if he wished he could have his telephone in his room at any time and he could use the pay station on the ward at any time. Concerning the security measures if you would like those in more detail, we began relaxing them. I first eased the regulations as a test on the twenty-sixth of April but found that the patient was not ready for it and that resulted in an order on the twenty-ninth of April that the watch was to remain in the room at all times, that the patient was still quite suicidal. The relaxation on the afternoon watch was only a few days later, on May first, which indicates how abruptly his condition would change at times in these undulating moments in the illness. I allowed the special watch to be out of the room from the evening meal until twenty-one hundred beginning the first of May. Five days later

we left the door open into the patient's room because of the heat in Mister Forrestal's room. On the seventh of May we allowed the day watch to relax somewhat and an order of that date states that the watch need not remain in the room at all times. It is impossible to put into writing what a special watch needs to know in detail; usually the men were always instructed personally, either by Doctor _____ or myself over and above the written order and this was simply authorization in writing for them to be out. We actually encouraged him to leave his room. It was not our assumption that he would be wandering around the hospital at two o'clock in the morning, that was his own idea. He ordinarily slept with the aid of sodium amytal right through the night and on Friday night I had been told by the resident that he slept through the night without medication. He was in that stage of improvement. He was very close to well actually. When I saw him on the eighteenth I felt we could, didn't tell him, but felt hospitalization for another thirty days would probably do the trick. He was that close to the end of it. That, of course, is the most dangerous time in any depression.

12. Q. What date did you leave Washington and turn the case over to Doctor _____ ?
    A. On May eighteenth. I should say that throughout the conduct of the case while I was in full charge and had full responsibility for it, it was a joint effort by four of us because I didn't feel that any one person could possibly find his way through that entire matter. As a result of this there was a morning conference with Doctor _____ Doctor _____ and myself each day. In addition, _____ came out in the beginning, twice, looked over the situation. I talked over the course of therapy with him and he concurred in it. I subsequently saw him around May first, the exact date I am not sure of, went over the case with him again and he felt that it was moving along about as was expected.

13. Q. Those residents that were on the port and starboard; were they there in case of emergency or did they have a routine of visiting the patient during the night?
    A. They were there primarily for the evening sick call, to be sure that medications, orders, were carried out and in event he needed anything; not limited to emergencies. The night time was a bad time with him always and the two residents were fully as aware of of his case and how to handle the things he would bring up. His depression began to get deeper in the late evening and very frequently he needed someone to talk to and I felt he had enough of me during the day and there should be someone else during that time. During my absence _____ spent some afternoons with him in interview but not with any very deep psychotherapy, simply superficial support.

14. Q. Did Mister Forrestal make any attempts at suicide while he was under your care?
    A. None whatsoever. The matter of suicide in Hobe Sound; he told Doctor _____ that he had attempted to hang himself with a belt. _____ and I were both very skeptical of that and both he and I were of the opinion it was sort of a nightmare. The man

-10-

had no marks on him and there was no broken belt. Very frequently a depressed person has a fantasy of dying and reports it as real. So far as I know he never made a single real attempt at suicide except that one that was successful. He was the type of individual, fast as lightening, of extremely high intelligence and one reason I doubt previous attempts I knew if he decided to do it he would do it and nobody would stop him. He was a boxer in college and his movements, even when depressed, were so quick you could hardly follow them with your eye. In the course of psychotherapy he talked a great deal about his suicide; he would tell me when he was feeling hopeless and had to do away with himself. At those times we would tighten restrictions. He would tell me in symbolic language. One morning he sent me a razor blade which he had concealed. When I interviewed him I said "What does this mean?". He said "It means I am not going to kill myself with a razor blade". Of course, he had the blade and could have done it. A man of that intelligence can kill himself at any time he desired and you can't very well stop him. He is my first personal suicide since nineteen thirty-six, thirteen years ago. The last one was on a locked ward at St. Elizabeth's Hospital under immediate supervision of an attendant. We discussed, whenever he felt badly enough, he would talk about the possibilities of killing himself and I am sure that when I left here on the eighteenth he had no intention at that time of harming himself.

15. Q. Had he, in the course of your interviews, either symbolically or otherwise, suggested his method if he committed suicide?
A. Yes, I am sure he didn't jump out of the window. My interviews with him were for one to three hours a day over a period of eight weeks; can't go into all the material that makes me think that but by the time he had been here four weeks I was certain there were only two methods he would use because he had told me, one was sleeping pills. He said that was the one way he could do it and the other was by hanging which made us feel somewhat more comfortable about the period of risk, knowing that he wasn't going out one of the windows. I haven't gone into all the details of what happened, but personally feel he tried to hang himself. I don't think he jumped; he may have; don't think it was out the window; think he meant to hang. For some time he had had complete access to the open windows in the residents' room and for a short period of time he even slept in there for two or three nights. There were two beds in the residents' room and he would sleep in one of those until about three o'clock and then go back to his own bed. That was the one thing that puzzled me, when he called me, as to what had happened; I couldn't believe it because of the window, until I got back and found out about the bathrobe cord.

16. Q. Would you tell us, Captain   the nature of the watch that was maintained in Mister Forrestal's room?
A. It was a psychiatric watch. I didn't know the corpsman who was on watch at the time of the suicide. However, I left the selection of the corpsmen entirely up to Doctor   and Doctor   who knew them personally much better than I. All of our men have had training in psychiatric safeguards and procedures although only very few of them are certified psychiatric technicians. We conduct a course of our own which runs for six months. I don't know how long the man on watch had even been here or whether he had had all of that course but know he must have been considered satisfactory to Doctor   or he wouldn't have been on watch.

-11-

17. Q. How many times did Doctor _____ visit at the hospital?
    A. Twice. He was here April third and April sixth.

18. Q. Will you please state Doctor _____ qualifications briefly?
    A. Doctor _____ is one of the most prominent psychiatrists in the country. He is just completing a term as the President of the American Psychiatric Association, the American Psychoanalytic Association and the Central Neuropsychiatric Association, probably the only man in history to hold all three offices simultaneously. He has so many governmental appointments as consultant that I don't know all of them; on the training committee of Public Health Service, hundreds of them, Veterans Committee of National Research Council, etc. Incidentally, for the information of the board, I was with Doctor _____ at the time I was notified of Mister Forrestal's death. His attitude was that it was the type of casualty which comes with therapeutic psychiatry; he knew all of the steps that had to be taken. I spent about thirty minutes with him on Sunday morning after the suicide; reviewed the case and he felt that the conduct of the case had been in accord with the principles which had been followed throughout. As a matter of fact, I also have a large number of telegrams and telephone calls from some twenty to thirty psychiatrists throughout the country, including Braceland _____ is Chief of Psychiatry at Mayo Clinic, beside the people here on my staff and Doctor _____ was the only other individual that knew in detail the conduct of the case. He was a personal friend of Mister Forrestal's and thought very highly of him and I had spent two days with _____ on May nineteenth and twentieth, and during that time had brought him up to date on the course of Mister Forrestal's case. He was at that point in complete accord with what we were doing and called last night, unfortunately I was out, but left word that he would be happy to appear if it were necessary, which was what Doctor _____ said - if the board of investigation would like to talk to him he would come down. I would personally hesitate to ask Doctor _____ to come until the end of the week because he is in charge of the meeting of American Psychiatric Association which is having some internal trouble and really should not be here but I am certain if the board wanted a telephonic communication with him he would be glad to help out any way he could.

19. Q. Did Doctor _____, at any time, discuss, suggest or agree on the relaxation of safety precautions when the time was appropriate?
    A. Yes, sir, we spent a great deal of time talking about the danger period and in trying particularly to find some way of transition from complete strict security to recovery. Mister Forrestal's prominence was such that it imposed a great burden on trying to make any arrangements in which he could have some freedom of movement. Literally hundreds of people who called about him, who knew about him, and some of those were friends, others were people whose primary interest seemed to be in what they could get out of him. He wasn't in any position to be exposed to any exploitations by crack pots, screwballs and what nots and _____ and I, and the family and I, and Mister _____ and I, at various times did

a great deal of discussing as to what the move would be in this
period of relaxation, how we would get him out of the hospital.
I personally, my personal plans were, within the period after I
came back, depending on his condition, to move him to tower
seventeen where there are no security screens at all and to
continue his watch about as it was being continued at the time I
left, or more an attending basis than a basis of very strict
supervision. It was this period that we were all worried about,
as to how it could be accomplished and   and I fully
agreed that restrictions would have to be removed as rapidly as
the patient's condition justified. The only hope for recovery in
people of that sort is to allow them to gradually take up
socialization activities. The confinement of a man to strict
isolation routine when he is depressed is very apt to fix the
illness; there has to be something to break him away from himself
and get him interested in the world outside and people outside.
From the very first Mister Forrestal's mail and other communications were handed to him unopened. He was allowed to see all
of them on the theory no one can live in a vacuum and might just
as well be exposed to whatever came along; that is the method of
dealing with it; it would depend on how well he was or how sick he
was. It was as simple as that. Actually, he dealt quite well
with almost everything. It is my own feeling from what I know
that the period of despondency which caused him to end his life
was very sudden in onset and probably the whole matter was on an
impulsive basis. That was the one thing I had feared, knowing of
his impulsivity. Again I say he moved like lightening, some of
those on pure impulse. That is supported by several things. I
talked to Doctor _   last night and was glad to hear him
say spontaneously and not just in agreement with me that he felt
that this was an impulsive thing of sudden origin, but one of the
main evidences is the complete absence of any suicidal note or
expression of suicidal intent in any way. He left no message at
all except this poem which I am sure was meant for me and was not
a portion of the suicide. That is to say, I think he was
simply writing that out to demonstrate how badly he felt. People
who contemplate suicide almost invariably leave some note to
someone and usually someone close. The absence of some note would
make me feel this was a very impulsive act of the moment. Mister
Forrestal was still being carried Under DU Medical Observation
but the psychiatric diagnosis was reactive depression.
Clinically, the depression was of mixed type but in the present
nomenclature the best diagnostic term applicable is Reactive
Depression. There were very strong reactive elements in it. It
is the type of depression which we saw very frequently during the
war; sixty to ninety day depressions in reaction to excessive
work or complete change in a man's life. He had reached a point
at which the entire life had to reoriented with giving up of his
job as Defense Secretary which he knew was coming some time back.
Everything had to be changed; his whole method of living which had
gone on for about nine years and at his age that sort of rearrange-
ment is a difficult task. Many people go through this sort of
thing in lesser degree. His, I think, was especially severe because he was worn out.

20. Q. Before he came to Bethesda while he was down south, did he make any attempt to slash his wrist?
    A. No, he had a small scratch on his wrist which he told me was not a suicidal attempt but he was considering it and he was wondering what he could do to himself and he took a knife or blade and scratched his wrist, so superficial it was not even dressed, and wouldn't come under the heading of "attempt" so far as I am concerned. There is one other thing about the treatment. We considered the possibility of electro-shock but felt that the reactive portion of the illness was so prominent that we should withhold electro-shock for at least ninety days. In reactive depressions if electro-shock is used early and the patient is returned to the same situation from which he came there is grave danger of suicide in the immediate period after they return. Of the last two or three people who have jumped from bridges in town here two of them, to my knowledge, were electro-shock cures of short duration, so strangely enough we left out electro-shock to avoid what actually happened anyhow.

Neither the recorder nor the members of the board desired further to examine this witness.

The board informed the witness that he was privileged to make any further statement covering anything relating to the subject matter of the investigation which he thought should be a matter of record in connection therewith, which had not been fully brought out by the previous questioning.

The witness made the following statement:

I would like to stress one point and that is that the responsibility of the case was entirely with me. I had nothing but the most complete cooperation from the hospital authorities here, from Mister Forrestal's friends, and from his family. I shared the conduct of the case with selected members of the staff because I needed their assistance but all of the direction of the case and the complete control of it was entirely in my hands. I would like to make that a matter of record. The problem of responsibility, the responsibility for its conduct was entirely mine.

Neither the recorder nor the members of the board desired further to examine this witness.

The witness said that he had nothing further to state.

The witness was duly warned and withdrew.

A witness was called, entered, was duly sworn, and was informed of the subject matter of the investigation.

Examined by the recorder:

1. Q. State your name, rank and present station of duty.
   A. _____, Commander, Medical Corps, U. S. Navy. My station is Psychiatric Service; officer in charge of the officers' neuropsychiatric service, U. S. Naval Hospital, Bethesda, Maryland.

2. Q. How long have you been in psychiatry and what are your qualifications?
A. I have had a special interest in psychiatry since nineteen thirty-two in college and have pursued the study with additional interest ever since. Technically, the first formal medical training period was from June nineteen forty-six to June nineteen forty-seven as Executive Officer and Resident in Training at the U. S. Naval Medical Unit, U. S. Public Health Service Hospital, Fort Worth, Texas. From July, 1947 to the present time I have been serving in my present assignment as officer in charge of the neuropsychiatric service of this hospital. My official status is on the staff.

3. Q. Would you please tell the board all that you know relative to your participation in the treatment of the late James V. Forrestal?
A. Just prior to Doctor   departure on Wednesday, May eighteenth he had indicated to me that he would like me to take administrative charge while he was gone. In preparation for this the first time that I met Mister Forrestal was for the purpose of being introduced to him on Monday afternoon, the sixteenth of May. I next saw him on Tuesday morning along with Doctor   briefly and then I saw him alone again for brief periods on the mornings of Thursday, Friday and Saturday. My primary administrative role was to handle all incoming calls, to decide whether or not visitors who wished to see Mister Forrestal should be permitted to see him, to take up with him directly his choice of wanting to see any particular visitors and to handle any inquiries that came from outside on either a professional or personal basis on all matters relative to his case. Since Doctor   had been in more complete and earlier contact with the case and Doctor   knew the case it was felt that he should continue to deal with the more personal aspects of the case and Doctor   and I conferred at various times regarding Mister Forrestal's condition. The feeling that I had regarding his condition, based upon my own observations and conferences with Doctor   was that his condition remained essentially the same. Most of my conversations with him were on a more or less impersonal nature with no serious attempt to enter into the actual therapeutic situation. I last saw Mister Forrestal on Saturday morning about ten o'clock at which time he seemed to be about the same as he had been on the preceding few mornings. About zero two ten Sunday morning I received a phone call from Doctor   in which he informed me that Mister Forrestal had gone through the window and his body was found below. Then called Doctor   in Montreal, Canada, and informed him of the situation and told him that I would come to the hospital immediately to do whatever was required.

Examined by the board:
4. Q. Doctor, during your period of supervision of this case was it necessary for you to change or issue any new orders?
A. No, sir, I considered his condition to remain essentially the same and made no change of any of the existent orders.

5. Q. When you took over charge of Mister Forrestal were you familiar with the various aspects of his case?
A. Yes, sir, in a rather general way. I had a general understanding of his over-all clinical picture, although I had had no active participation in the case up to Monday, May sixteenth.

6. Q. Were you aware of the possibility of suicide?
   A. Yes, sir.

7. Q. You stated that he was about the same; over what period of time did you have reference to, did you mean from the time he entered the hospital or for the few days you were cognizant of his case?
   A. That would only be from the period the first time I saw him on Monday the sixteenth up to Saturday the twenty-first.

8. Q. Saturday was the last time you saw him?
   A. Yes, sir.

9. Q. What time?
   A. Approximately ten o'clock Saturday morning.

10. Q. And you saw no change in his condition at that time; no evidence of any undue disturbance or agitation or depression?
    A. No, sir, he continued his usual discussions; he was rather brief in his discussions. It was rather difficult to reach him in a sense of establishing a close personal contact but his intellectual functionings seemed as usual. He gave no increased evidence of tension or depressive features; made no unusual references. Most of our discussions were conversations either of personal life, he usually directing questions toward me about my activities, or some of my background features but since I was not entering into the treatment situation I saw no reason for participating in personal discussions.

11. Q. Then you saw no reason whatsoever to make any change in orders, to tighten up on security or take extra precautions?
    A. That is correct.

12. Q. Doctor, in the preliminary testimony you stated that there was a dual function, that you, Doctor _____ were to handle the incoming inquiries and Doctor _____, because he was better acquainted with this case, to handle the professional aspect. In other words, Doctor _____ handled the professional and you handled the administrative matters?
    A. That is essentially true but at the same time the over-all responsibility was mine since I was placed in charge of his case and I conferred for that reason with Doctor _____ as to his opinions of the more personal phase of the patient's condition.

13. Q. But you actually didn't have any psychiatric interviews with Mister Forrestal?
    A. Not more than would be derived from conversations I had with him on the mornings of Thursday, Friday and Saturday.

14. Q. Did Mister Forrestal make any attempt at suicide while you had charge of the patient?
    A. No, sir, none that I was ever informed of, became aware of, or suspected.

15. Q. Did Mister Forrestal indicate in any way to you that he might do harm to himself?
    A. None whatever.

16. Q. Doctor _____, if you had - in your observations of this case and in the absence of Doctor _____ who was in immediate charge, would you have felt free to change any safety precautions that might be taken?
A. Yes, sir, it was understood between Doctor _____ and I if there was any question in the condition of the patient which required any further consideration or attention to get in touch with him immediately.

17. Q. To get in touch with him or take immediate action?
A. I would have assumed either way; if immediate action was indicated I would have felt free to take it or if I had any other questions about it I would have felt free to contact him.

18. Q. But you saw no indication at any time to take action or change any orders?
A. No, sir, I saw no specific indication for changing the course of management or treatment.

19. Q. There was a hospital corpsman on watch on Mister Forrestal, was there not?
A. Yes, sir.

20. Q. But he was not required to be in the room?
A. Not at all times at this stage.

21. Q. Did he have orders to check up on him every so often?
A. His orders were to be with the patient most of the time but that he could leave the room as desired for purposes which were indicated.

22. Q. Do you remember the man on watch between the midnight and two o'clock Sunday morning on the twenty-second?
A. Yes, sir, that was a corpsman by the name of _____

23. Q. Is he designated as a neuropsychiatric technician?
A. No, sir, but he had had a degree of training on the neuropsychiatric service in the closed wards which would be enough to give him sufficient understanding of this type of problem.

24. Q. Were you and Doctor _____ in full accord that the safety precautions were adequate at the time?
A. Yes, sir, based on my understanding of the case as derived from Captain _____ and my conversations with Doctor _____ that there had been no perceptible change in the patient's condition and also my own observation. I had observed no perceptible change in the patient's condition.

25. Q. You had had conversation with Doctor _____ about it, is that right?
A. Yes, sir.

26. Q. Is this corpsman that had the watch from after twelve o'clock - was he aware of the suicidal tendencies of Mister Forrestal and had he been instructed to watch against suicide?
A. To the best of my knowledge he had been informed of the nature of the case and written instructions for the corpsmen were detailed in the chart, and, in addition, there was a doctor in constant attendance at the spot where he could obtain any additional information or understanding as desired.

-17-

27. Q. Was Mister Forrestal permitted to go into the galley or the passageway of the sixteenth deck without supervision?
    A. It is my understanding that the restrictions had been lifted to a degree where he was permitted to go out to the passageway to make phone calls or to enter the doctors' room adjoining his.

28. Q. Did Mister Forrestal exhibit any abnormal behavior Saturday morning when you saw him?
    A. No, sir, none that seemed to me any more different from his usual attitude of the preceding mornings.

Neither the recorder nor the members of the board desired further to examine this witness.

The board informed the witness that he was privileged to make any further statement concerning the subject matter of the investigation which he thought should be a matter of record in connection therewith, which had not been fully brought out by the previous questioning.

The witness said that he had nothing further to state.

The witness was duly warned and withdrew.

The board then, at 12:04 p.m., took a recess until 1:15 p.m., at which time it reconvened.

Present: All the members, the recorder, and the reporter.

No witnesses not otherwise connected with the investigation were present.

A witness was called, entered, was duly sworn, and was informed of the subject matter of the investigation.

Examined by the recorder:

1. Q. State your name, rank and present station.
   A. _____ Commander, Medical Corps, U.S. Navy, presently attached to the U. S. Naval Hospital, Bethesda, Maryland.

2. Q. What are your duties at the Naval Hospital?
   A. My duties are - I am a resident in neuropsychiatry.

3. Q. How long have you been a neuropsychiatrist in this resident status?
   A. Since I reported to the Naval Hospital on October eighteenth, nineteen forty-six.

4. Q. Would you please tell the board all you know relative to your connection with the treatment of the late James V. Forrestal?
   A. My first knowledge of Mister Forrestal's case was on Sunday afternoon, April third, after his admission to this hospital on Saturday, at which time I was called at home by Captain _____ and told to report to the hospital that afternoon and be prepared to spend the night. I reported to the hospital and to Captain _____ and was informed that I was to stand a special watch, sleeping in the room adjacent to Mister Forrestal's suite and that my duties, so far as the watch was concerned, were to handle any emergency that might come up during my tour of duty at night and also to keep Doctors _____ and _____, who were handling the case, informed of what was going on. I continued to stand a regular watch at night with Mister Forrestal on alternate nights, to alternate with Doctor _____. The hours to be covered were from the end of working hours, approximately sixteen thirty, until the beginning of working hours the next morning at zero eight-thirty. In the mornings Doctor

-18-

would visit Mister Forrestal briefly and Doctor usually saw him in the afternoons. After Mister Forrestal was started on sub-shock insulin therapy my duties were increased to the extent that I was to report and remain in the room with the patient for the last thirty minutes of the insulin therapy period. This therapy period was usually started at eight o'clock and terminated at eleven hundred. So, on the days that he received insulin I was with him from approximately ten thirty to a few minutes after eleven hundred. After the insulin therapy was discontinued I went back to my old schedule of on every other night. When Doctor ____ left town he asked me to make a point of sitting with Mister Forrestal at some time during the day every day. This I took to mean in the afternoons at the times that Captain ___ had ordinarily been seeing him and on Wednesday, Thursday, Friday, ___ did sit with Mister Forrestal for anywhere from forty-five minutes to an hour and a half and sat with him briefly on Saturday morning. That about covers the whole time as to when I was actually here.

Examined by the board:

5. Q. Were you fully aware of the various phases of Mister Forrestal's condition from shortly after he was admitted as a patient to the hospital?
   A. Yes, sir, Doctor ____ Doctor ____ Doctor ____ and I had discussed at intervals various procedures and therapeutic efforts that were being made during the course of the entire case.

6. Q. During the period of his stay in the hospital did you feel that he was making some gradual improvement.
   A. Yes, sir, my feeling from the first was that he was pretty overly depressed, as evidenced by his lack of interest in his surroundings, interest in personal contact with me on the brief occasions that I saw him, whereas as the case progressed, particularly during the insulin period he seemed to become more alert, more interested in his surroundings, and particularly interested in what was going on about the floor itself and the hospital.

7. Q. What was your feeling in regard to the possibility of suicide during the first few days of his stay in the hospital?
   A. My feeling with regard to suicide during the first few days of his stay in the hospital was that it was potentially present, that being based on psychiatric experience with depressed patients. I had no actual factual evidence of any sort which would lead me to be able to say specifically that suicidal thoughts or ideas were present. However, I did feel and consider it a possibility on the basis of general psychiatric knowledge.

8. Q. What was your feeling in regard to the possibility of suicide at approximately the time that Doctor ____ left Washington?
   A. At that time I felt that Mister Forrestal had made a definite improvement in the over-all picture from the time of his admission and that the possibility of suicide was much more remote than earlier in the case. There were several observations made during the course of the case which led me to feel this. About two weeks before Doctor ____ left I went up to stand the watch one night and stopped by the room to speak to Mister Forrestal, asked him how he was feeling. He said "About as usual". We chatted briefly about my medical education and where I lived and what not; then later,

-19-

when I came up to go to bed about twenty-two forty-five, he was
awake and I asked him how he was feeling. He said "About as usual"
but he felt his room was a little stuffy and in view of the fact
that two of the windows were stuck and couldn't be opened I agreed
that the room was a little stuffy. He said that he thought possibly
he would be able to sleep better if he slept in the room with me, -
there being two beds in my bedroom and I said I thought that would
be a good idea, it might be more comfortable over there. So he did sleep
in the room that I slept in that night. My feelings at this time
were that the patient was making an effort to broaden his horizons.
I felt that he was lonely and felt the need of friendly contact
with other people and also felt the time that the suicidal possibilities had lessened sufficiently to make it safe for him to
remain out of his own room. The danger of suicide had been discussed with Doctors   and   on several occasions prior to
this and we had been encouraging the patient to broaden his
activities even prior to this particular incident.

9. Q. At any time while Doctor   was away did he appear to you to be
preoccupied, worried, disturbed or agitated more than usual?
A. To the contrary, he appeared less preoccupied, worried, disturbed,
and particularly less agitated. On Wednesday afternoon after
Doctor   left Wednesday morning I stayed with him about an
hour. The relationship during that hour was as usual. We talked
of superficial things such as the flowers in his room, a thorn I
had removed from his thumb some time previously. Thursday night he
said that he would like to attempt sleeping without his usual medication of sodium amytal and I agreed to that with him for a trial
period but insisted that if he were not asleep within a reasonable
length of time, I think about an hour, he should take his amytal.
On Friday I sat with him for about an hour Friday afternoon. He
was slightly more cheerful than he had been on Thursday. The impression that I had of him on Thursday was identical with the impression I had with him on the Sunday before which was a day that
Captain   didn't see him. That is to say, his appearance and
my feeling for his condition was almost identical.

10. Q. Did you, at any time during Doctor   ' absence, discuss his
condition with Doctor   ?
A. Yes, sir, we talked over almost everything that happened with
Doctor   and Doctor

11. Q. During this period did anything come up that made you think that you
should tauten up on his privileges any?
A. No, sir, to the contrary. The things that did come up, the feeling
I had was if anything, privileges should be extended. We didn't
increase any privileges during this period because we didn't have
Captain   or Captain   aboard to discuss the matter and we
figured we would let the standing orders that they had left when they
left remain. However, those orders were, we felt, relatively lenient
and that Mister Forrestal was fully capable and able to go along on
that line without any change either to increase or to decrease the
restrictions that were in effect at that time.

-20-

12. Q. Did you see him Saturday, May twenty-first?
    A. Yes, sir, I saw him.

13. Q. Give us your impressions of him at that time.
    A. Saturday morning when I woke up, having slept in the room next to his with both the doors opened through the bathroom with my bed arranged so that I could look directly into his room and he could look directly in my room, I got up, dressed, went in and spoke to him, asked him the kind of night he had. That night, Friday night, he had slept the entire night with no awakening periods that I know of at all without a sedative. On Friday night he had gone to bed while I was in the room sitting with him. While I was sitting with him Friday night he said he felt sleepy and got in bed. Shortly after he had been in bed for a little while I left and checked with the corpsman about nine o'clock to find out had he taken his amytal. The corpsman said he was sleeping so I said "Well, don't wake him up to give him some amytal." My understanding was that he slept the entire night.

14. Q. What was your final impression of him when you left him Saturday?
    A. I saw him again Saturday morning at which time an old friend of his from New York came down to visit, a Mister   . We had been informed by Captain   on Thursday night that Mister   would be down Saturday morning and he had permission to visit. I had told Mister Forrestal on Friday afternoon that Mister   would be down Saturday morning. He had no comment. My impression Saturday morning was that his condition was about as it had been for the last several days. He didn't appear to be particularly depressed, neither did he appear to be particularly cheerful.

15. Q. Then you left him Saturday feeling very comfortable about his condition?
    A. Saturday noon I spoke to Doctor   as he was taking over the week-end watch and told Doctor   that I felt the week-end coming up would be about as usual which was my feeling and considered the possibility of dropping back by Sunday afternoon to sit with him as I had been doing but decided, on the basis of the fact that I felt he was getting along alright, that that would not be necessary and didn't plan to come over on Sunday afternoon to sit with him.

16. Q. Did Mister Forrestal, in the times you would be with him, express anything about international affairs, discuss them with you?
    A. No, sir.

17. Q. Do you think he was trying to get away from such things?
    A. I didn't have much feeling about whether he was or not. He never made any effort to talk along those lines when I was with him, no, sir. In fact, the basis of most of our conversations were relatively superficial, having to do with things of the moment; should he take his sleeping pills or not; was I going to sleep in the room next to him or not; how was the rose thorn in his finger getting along; or whether his constipation was being taken care of or not. Another one of my duties in the case was to write orders for his bowels and I had done that earlier in the course of the case.

-21-

18. Q. During your conversations with him did he show any interest in discussing any current events or anything outside of himself?
A. Only once. He asked me on several occasions did I plan to remain in the service and I remarked once that I planned to remain in the service if the service treated me as well as it had in the past but with all of the changes in prospect relative to the Navy and the services I was standing by to see how some of those came out and keeping an open mind on the subject. He evidenced considerable interest at that time saying that he had been in on the unification deal and said that he felt that it was a good thing and would probably work out to everyone's advantage. This was said in a rather round-about fashion and not specifically a direct quote. I don't remember the exact words.

19. Q. Did he ever discuss any of the lighter things like baseball?
A. He discussed briefly golfing with me once, merely to say that he had been a golfer at one time and that's about all so far as the lighter things were concerned.

20. Q. Were the windows in Mister Forrestal's room locked on the Saturday morning that you last saw him?
A. Two of them were unlocked, two locked.

21. Q. Could those windows be opened to permit a person to go out though these windows?
A. No, the window screens on Mister Forrestal's room were; there were a total of four security screens. In the room itself three screens, two on one side, one on one side, fourth in the head. In the installation of the security screens the two screens nearest his bed were warped and couldn't be opened or closed without getting a part of the scale that was in the room and taking two people to prize and push and twist to open and close it. I know this because the corpsman and I tried one of them out about a week or week and a half before the case ended. In the entire area the overhead drops down about eighteen inches in front of the windows which were offset. These security screens open inward and hit on this overhead long before they can be opened and when we opened these two they were warped. One afternoon to raise the windows - it was a sultry day, one of the thunderstorm afternoons - the corpsman that was on, quite a small fellow, and I were working on it and I remember distinctly trying to get him to get behind the screen on the window side to try to raise the windows and he couldn't get in there and following this I didn't see any point in locking the two warped frames because their purpose of guarding the window was answered whether they were locked or unlocked; namely, they couldn't be opened sufficiently for even a small person to get out even if they were unlocked. There were no security screens in the doctors' bedroom and for a period of two or three weeks the door from the head to the doctors' room had been left unlocked and frequently wide open to improve the ventilation in Mister Forrestal's room. I tried to encourage him to move about the area after the general feeling among the staff was that his horizons needed to be broadened.

22. Q. At the time that you left him Saturday morning, May twenty-first, did you notice that the ashtray or Petri plate was broken in Mister Forrestal's room?
A. To the contrary. I noticed that the ashtray Petri plate was not broken before because I recall distinctly using it for my cigarette while I was in there. That had been my usual ashtray when I went in. He had another one by the bed.

Neither the recorder nor the members of the board desired further to examine this witness.

The board informed the witness that he was privileged to make any further statement covering anything relating to the subject matter of the investigation which he thought should be a matter of record in connection therewith, which had not been fully brought out by the previous questioning.

The witness made the following statement:

My impression of the entire case was that Mister Forrestal was admitted to the hospital in a definitely depressed condition, was quite ill and that during the course of his stay in the hospital his improvement was gradually upward at all times with minor day-to-day fluctuations in mood. My viewpoint during the entire case was a hopeful one and in all my contacts with the patient what few efforts I made to talk with him were aimed along hopeful lines for a complete return to his normal way of life.

Re-examined by the board:

23. Q. Doctor, did you know the night corpsman who was on duty with Mister Forrestal Saturday night extending into Sunday morning?
    A. Yes, sir.

24. Q. What was his name?
    A. His name was   .

25. Q. Did you regard him as being a suitable and competent watch for Mister Forrestal during those hours?
    A. Yes, sir.

The board did not desire further to examine this witness.

The board informed the witness that he was privileged to make any further statement covering anything relating to the subject matter of the investigation which he thought should be a matter of record in connection therewith, which had not been fully brought out by the previous questioning.

The witness said that he had nothing further to state.

The witness was duly warned and withdrew.

A witness was called, entered, was duly sworn, and was informed of the subject matter of the investigation.

Examined by the recorder:

1. Q. State your name, rank and present station.
    A. Commander   , Medical Corps, U. S. Navy, U. S. Naval Hospital, Bethesda, Maryland.

2. Q. What are your duties at the Naval Hospital?
    A. Resident in second year training in psychiatry.

3. Q. What is your experience in training in neuropsychiatry?
    A. I have been in residency status since December nineteen forty-seven when I reported here at Bethesda. Since that time I have been continually on the psychiatric service except for three months last fall when I was on neurology and I am at present again on neurology, having been on neurology since April first, nineteen forty-nine.

4. Q. Will you please tell the board all you know relative to your connection with the late Mister Forrestal?
   A. When Mister Forrestal first came to the hospital as a patient I was designated as one of the two residents to stand night calls, you might say. We were instructed by Doctor _____ that we would be on hand any time we were needed and that we should sleep in the room which adjoined the room of Mister Forrestal. The watch, or call, both apply, began on _____ days we had the call at four-thirty and extended through next morning until eight-thirty. On weekends, we split it port and starboard, would have week-end duty beginning at twelve noon on Saturday extending through 'til eight-thirty on Monday. Our duties were primarily to be at hand if any question arose in the carrying out of the orders that were written for Mister Forrestal, to give assistance to the corpsman or nurse if they so desired, to make our routine rounds and visit the patient and on any matter which we didn't feel qualified to handle (I am referring to Doctor _____ when I say "we") we were to get in contact with either Doctor _____ or with Doctor _____. The past week since Doctor _____ was away Doctor _____ had been designated as the administrative officer-in-charge and in case of any difficulties during that period, the period when we couldn't contact Doctor _____ or _____ we were supposed to get in touch with Doctor _____

5. Q. When was the beginning of that watch with reference to date?
   A. I can't say for sure so far as the date goes but Mister Forrestal came to the hospital on a Saturday. Doctor _____ had the first duty on Sunday night and I had the duty on Monday night; one of the first week-ends in April but so far as definite day I am not sure.

6. Q. That watch has been continuous since that time up until this past Saturday night, is that right?
   A. Yes, sir.

Examined by the board:

7. Q. Were you fully aware of the various phases of Mister Forrestal's condition?
   A. I was not aware of anything that went on in therapy but I was informed and from my own observation had what I thought was a fairly good knowledge of his condition all the time.

8. Q. Did the matter of suicide ever occur to you?
   A. It certainly occurred to me ever since the man has been there.

9. Q. How did you regard him from that standpoint for the first few days of his stay in the hospital?
   A. Well, of course, on the first few days, it was much longer than the first few days, on admission to the hospital he was under almost continuous sedation and constant watch. After a few days they were able to get screened windows on the room and corpsmen were instructed to stay with Mister Forrestal at all times and if they needed anything from the nurse or corpsman on the outside or from Doctor _____ and me they went through another corpsman, didn't leave the room at any time. Following that he was on sub-shock insulin therapy for a period of something like three weeks, I believe, and the man was obviously depressed and any time a man is depressed there is always a consideration of suicide to be kept in mind.

-24-

10. Q. How did you regard the progress of his condition from the time of admission to the hospital until the time that Doctor   left town?

    A. Well, I think it is best to put it this way. From discussions with Doctor   , Doctor   and Doctor   and from the changes in the orders which permitted Mister Forrestal to have more freedom of movement in that he could go into our bedroom and he could be in the room alone without the corpsman I presumed, I felt that improvement was going along or those measures would not have been put into effect. So far as my personal dealing with Mister Forrestal on his original entry and at the time he was on insulin therapy it was always quite difficult to talk with Mister Forrestal, quite difficult because we had been instructed to try to stay away from things that were on therapy and for a man like Mister Forrestal you couldn't very well talk to him about the flowers and bees because he was not interested in them. I could ask questions about his Navy life and that sort of thing but always felt that would be getting into a field I should not be in, the psychotherapeutic field, and for that reason I say I found it difficult to talk with him; would discuss things, primarily me, at his questioning but as time went on there was the opportunity to maybe discuss other things. Don't know just when it was but when Mister   in London had that accident he talked with me about that. From time to time he would ask me questions about was the duty difficult, was I working hard and so on and so forth so that during the period of time he was here in the hospital I felt he was showing continually more interest in outside activities but, as I said, in the beginning the way I looked at it I felt sure things were going on in discussion with Doctor   probably I didn't know about but which were indications that the man was improving considerably.

11. Q. You did, however, from objective signs form some opinion of your own that he was improving?

    A. Yes, sir, I did, the night that this happened. Doctor   had encouraged Doctor   and me to see if we could possibly get Mister Forrestal to go for a walk or maybe take him up to the television on the eighteenth floor and on Saturday two times, once about quarter of eight I asked him if he would be interested in going up to see the television and he said "No, thank you, I think I will let it go." Then again at eleven o'clock or thereabouts I talked with him again. The television, strictly speaking, I think is supposed to be closed around ten-thirty, but is sometimes on a little later. When I came up to go to bed some time before eleven I asked him again if he would be interested in going to the television and he said "No, not tonight.", but he made it sound like not tonight but a night near in the future I will go up with you.

12. Q. During Doctor   absence did you observe anything that made you think his privileges should be tautened up?

    A. No, sir, I didn't observe a thing.

13. Q. Did you discuss at any time his condition with Doctor   or Doctor   ?

    A. Saturday noon, May twenty-first, when I went on watch I saw Doctor   in the chow hall and Doctor   just having come off Thursday and Friday nights was pleased that he had the week-end free and said to me "You will have an easy time of it, everything is going along fine." That was the extent of any discussion. I knew Doctor   had talked with Mister Forrestal on Saturday morning, May twenty-first, and there was very little discussion between us. If he said anything it was of so little importance I forgot what it was.

-25-

14. Q. Saturday night, May twenty-first when you went to bed how did you feel about Mister Forrestal's condition?

    A. When I got up on tower sixteen I talked with the corpsman who was on duty. He told me that Mister Forrestal had been resting off and on all evening but that he still hadn't taken his medication. I told the corpsman that I felt possibly my coming to bed would have some bearing on whether Mister Forrestal went to sleep or not and I thought he probably would go to bed and stay in bed after I came up. At no time has there been, in the past three weeks, any hard and fast rule about whether or not Mister Forrestal should take his sleeping medication although it was always ordered, the reason being that at least since I knew Mister Forrestal he had always complained that he didn't like the sensation of the medication and always wanted to try to sleep without the medication. I viewed his taking or not taking medication just another indication of his gradual improvement and sort of a stepping-stone to further good health. For that reason at no time did I ever insist that Mister Forrestal would take the nightly medication but on numerous occasions I knew that even though he took his amytal he still would be up maybe one or two times during the night going into the bathroom or at least not sleeping. When I had the duty on Wednesday, the eighteenth of May, I went up about seven-thirty to make my evening rounds. Mister Forrestal was asleep, he hadn't taken any medication and when I went up again to go to bed in the neighborhood of eleven-thirty he was still sleeping so that was proof enough for me he was able to sleep without taking nightly medication.

15. Q. Can you tell us a little more specifically your impression and what happened on the last night that you had the duty, which was Saturday, May twenty-first?

    A. I mentioned previously that when I went up on tower sixteen around eleven the corpsman had mentioned that Mister Forrestal had not been sleeping and then I also previously mentioned that I had discussion with the corpsman at that time. I went in to see Mister Forrestal and that was the time I discussed again with him the possibility of going up and seeing the television. He implied not that night but in the future. I again reminded him if he were not sleeping and could not get to sleep he should take his medications, to which he answered "I will." For the past, I think it was the second of May I would have to check the record to make sure, since that time the adjoining bathroom door into my room has been left open from time to time. That particular night while we were talking about the television and his taking the medication he said "Are you going to close the door" and I said "Yes, because it is cold and I don't want to catch another cold. I had had a cold for a couple weeks previously and he knew about it and that was one of our subjects of conversation from time to time and he said that perfectly alright or something like that so I went into my room, got undressed, went into the bathroom, came back, read the newspaper for a while and from here on in I'm not sure of any times but I would presume that I possibly went to bed about eleven thirty. I wasn't sleeping and although I realized that these lessening of restrictions on the patient were a part of the treatment in his road to recovery, frankly, at times I was ill at ease about the fact that there were two open windows in my bedroom. Whether or not you realize that some restrictions are relaxed, that some risks have to be taken, I don't think that removes the concern from the people who might be involved in those risks. This was something that had been discussed with both Doctor   and Doctor   Some nights the door would be locked, other nights the door would be closed, another night the door would be opened but on that particular night the door was closed when I

-26-

went to bed but as I was lying in bed at one time I heard a little sort of thud and didn't know whether the wind was coming through Mister Forrestal's room and banging the door or venetian blinds banging against the window but anyhow I stayed awake just a short period of time and while I was awake Mister Forrestal walked into my room, stood in front of the window next to the bathroom door, looked out for a half-second, turned around, went back through the bathroom into his room and left the door open. I got up and walked over beside the other bed so I could look into the room and Mister Forrestal was lying in his bed. I got back into the bed again and then I started thinking that, well, I told him the door was supposed to be closed, he's got the door open, now should I get up and close it or shouldn't I. I finally decided with the air swishing through and the banging of the door I probably wouldn't get to sleep at all unless I closed it so I got up to close it and was standing in front of the bathroom door with my back to the door which by that time was about three-quarters shut, I presume from the wind blowing it, and just as I was reaching to the knob to close the door Mister Forrestal, who was evidently standing in the bathroom, I didn't see him but we had a few words. He said "Are you going to lock the door" and I said "Yes, because the wind is coming up and it will be banging and it is getting cold here in my room" and he said "Well," I'm not sure but something like well, that's alright and then I said "Haven't you been sleeping?" He said "Yes, off and on" and I said again "You better take your medication you need the sleep, it will do you good" and he said "Alright I will." I locked the door, lit a cigarette and was standing there in the dark smoking the cigarette and thought - well, I'll see if there's something else in the paper I haven't read. I turned the light on, put my white coat on - I use it as a sort of bathrobe - and started out to the nurse's desk to get a drink of water. Just as I went by the galley Mister Forrestal and one of the corpsmen were standing in the galley door. As I went out to the desk I watched him going back into his room with the corpsman. I got no drink of water, came back into my room, read the paper for about three minutes and got back in bed. I didn't have the slightest idea what time it was; didn't hear anything else or wasn't concerned about anything else. The light in the galley went on a couple of times but that's not unusual and the next thing I knew was the corpsman, came in, awakened me and said that Mister Forrestal still was not sleeping, what should he do about it. I said something like this - that Mister Forrestal knew that he should take his pills if he were unable to sleep without them and that the corpsman should again remind him that the pills were there and that he should take them if he felt he couldn't go to sleep by himself. At the same time I told the corpsman to keep a close eye on Mister Forrestal. I don't know what time that was but after all this happened and in talking with the corpsman and nurse I think it was about one thirty-five or something like that when the corpsman came and talked to me. I went back to sleep again because the next thing I recall was Miss   coming into the room; she flipped the light on, don't know which I was conscious of first and she said "Mister Forrestal is not in his room." I sat up in bed and as I sat up the first thing that flashed through my mind was that he was wandering around the passageway somewhere and I said "Where is he" and she said "I think he's out the window" so I quickly got up and by the time I was dressed everybody had been shocked about this thing but you can imagine how shocked I was. I went out once to the nurse's desk in my white coat without any pants on and then came back into my room to get dressed. By that time there were numerous and sundry and many people, including the Officer-of-the-Day, Doctor   and I had gone in the galley and looked out the window and saw him down there and then I went to the desk and called Doctor   to tell him what had happened. Doctor

-27-

said "Does the Officer-of-the-Day know about it" and I said "Yes, he has just been up here but now that I have called you I will go down to see if he has notified Admiral   ."

16. Q. When you retired for the night did you believe that any closer restriction should be exercised?
    A. No, sir, I didn't.

17. Q. Was it usual for Mister Forrestal to get up during the night and to walk around or was that an unusual happening on the night in question?
    A. In the previous things I have said I hoped to convey the idea I didn't think any of his activities that night were unusual in any respect. I knew nights he had a capsule and slept, nights he had capsules and didn't sleep, nights that he slept without anything. It was not unusual for him in the middle of the night to get up, walk over into our room and walk back into his room. As a matter of fact, on, well, two nights with Doctor   . I think and one night I am sure of with me, Mister Forrestal asked if he could come over and sleep in the empty bed in our room which we permitted and discussed with Doctor   . Doctor   said "It is perfectly alright, the man is lonely and dependent and if you people don't mind its perfectly alright." On the nights that he didn't do that he would, say on at least two occasions when I had the duty, he would come into my room, stand in the door and walk back into his own room. Other nights I have heard him in the middle of the night, three o'clock in the morning or something like that, in the bathroom and I could see nothing unusual, nothing different in the way that he had acted on many previous occasions.

Neither the recorder nor the members of the board desired further to examine this witness.

The board informed the witness that he was privileged to make any further statement covering anything relating to the subject matter of the investigation which he thought should be a matter of record in connection therewith, which had not been fully brought out by the previous questioning.

The witness made the following statement:

I think I have mentioned before but would like to add again that I was conscious of the fact that Mister Forrestal had not completely recovered. I was also conscious of the fact if we expected any recovery whatsoever the only way it would be brought about would be by gradual relaxation of the restrictions under which the patient had been originally subjected. In all depressed people there is that chance that has to be taken. It doesn't leave a lot of people very happy about it but at the same time it is the only thing that can be done I feel in allowing the patient to gradually return to a previous better state of well being.

Neither the recorder nor the members of the board desired further to examine this witness.

The witness said that he had nothing further to state.

The witness was duly warned and withdrew.

A witness was called, entered, was duly sworn, and was informed of the subject matter of the investigation.

-28-

by the recorder:

1. Q. State your name, rank, and present station of duty.
   A. _____, Captain, Medical Corps, U. S. Naval Reserve, my station is U. S. Naval Hospital, Bethesda, Maryland.

2. Q. What are your duties at the Naval Hospital?
   A. I am assistant chief of the Psychiatric Service.

3. Q. Will you give a resume of your qualifications as a psychiatrist?
   A. I graduated from Tufts College Medical School in nineteen twenty, interned at Boston City Hospital. During the succeeding twenty-nine years I have spent a major portion of that time in the active practice of psychiatry. Among other positions which I have held are Physician in Charge of the Philadelphia Hospital for Mental Diseases; Clinical Director of the Polk State School in Polk, Pennsylvania; Medical Director of Halbrook Sanitorium, Greens Farms, Connecticut; U. S. Navy from April forty-two to August forty-six at which time I returned to the private practice of psychiatry in Westport, Connecticut, and returned to temporary active duty in the Navy September tenth, nineteen forty-eight. I am a Member of the American Psychiatric Association; the New York Society for Clinical Psychiatry; the Connecticut Psychiatric Society; for the past approximately fifteen years I have been an instructor in psychiatry at the College of Physicians and Surgeons at Columbia University, New York City. I am consulting psychiatrist to the Norwalk Hospital, Norwalk, Connecticut; Grace New Haven Hospital, New Haven, Connecticut; Stamford Hall in Stamford, Connecticut; on military leave from the indicated hospital appointments and at the present time I am also assistant Clinical Professor of Psychiatry at Georgetown University. I was also formerly on the teaching staff at the Medical School at Yale.

4. Q. Captain, will you please tell the board what you know relative to the treatment of the late Mister Forrestal?
   A. Perhaps I should begin by saying that the treatment was directed by Captain _____ who is the chief of the neuropsychiatric service and my role was supportive to his therapeutic endeavors and consultive at any time when it was deemed necessary or advisable. I first met Mister Forrestal on the day of his admission to the hospital which, I believe, was April second and subsequently saw him almost daily until May eighteenth at which time I left on authorized leave and didn't return until after his demise. Through Doctor _____ and through my daily conversation with the patient I acquired some degree of familiarity with the emotional state which was responsible for his hospitalization. I found him to be a very cooperative patient and at all times quite willing to accept opinions concerning his illness and an expressed willingness on his part to avail himself of all the benefits which might be derived from his hospitalization here and the psychotherapeutic therapy which might be instituted. In the nature of our handling of his psychotherapeutic therapy it was an arrangement between Doctor _____ and myself that he would completely control all the therapeutic measures although I can sincerely state that we compared opinions almost daily, particularly in regard to the behavior reactions of the patient and their import. Inasmuch as it is considered good psychiatric practice to avoid confliction and confusion in treatment, especially as it pertains to the interpretation of psychodynamics, that this rests entirely in the hands of one individual. As a result of this arrangement my discussions with Mister

-29-

Forrestal were on a less personal level than would accrue from therapeutic endeavors. However, these conversations had a degree of intimacy and resulted in the establishment of a rapport with Mister Forrestal that I always interpreted as being friendly and comfortable. He talked of many diverse matters that had only a casual relationship to his illness as he was a man who not only was mentally alert but continued to maintain an active interest in all current matters on a level compatible with his broad public service and wide experience. These conversations ran a gamut from a discussion of matters of purely local interest to various philosophies and ruminations that touched on the behavior patterns of all people under various circumstances of stress and his astuteness and acumen were such that his comments and discourses were pregnant with comprehensive significance. As indicated previously, the matter of discussion of the more intimate aspects of his personal problems was left for his interviews with Doctor   This Mister Forrestal and I both understood; that this was the arrangement and for that reason our tendency was to stay on less disturbing subjects. My interviews with him usually would last from fifteen or twenty minutes to perhaps an hour. In evaluating the course of his illness as I observed it he apparently was showing continuous improvement with moderate fluctuations which were not incompatible with the type of emotional disturbance which he showed. He was acutely aware of his depressed state of mind and at times asserted interpretation of his own reaction to his predicament and situations which might have led up to it although he not infrequently mentioned impending disaster. They were always of vague and non-specific character and had to do with matters which had always been of paramount interest to him, namely, the safety of the country. Many times he expressed uneasiness about the future possibilities and wondered whether or not people were as alert to these potentialities as they should be. Each time he would reassure himself by such assertions as, "I really have no uneasiness about the future of the country, I am certain that that is assured. But the travail might be easier if people perhaps were more concerned about some of these things." He talked frequently of his recovery and the possible change in his pattern of living which would be possible with more leisure and greater opportunity for diversification of interest and a release from the tremendous pressure which his duties had imposed on him over the preceding eight or nine years. He himself offered the opinion that he should have sensed that his burden had become too heavy many months previously and should have done something to correct it. He regretted that he hadn't done so. Incidentally, he, on several occasions in connection with this type of thinking had offered the opinion that all men highly placed in public life should be more concerned about their emotional health and even perhaps come to a better understanding of the benefits which would result from a more profound knowledge of the emotional concomitant of continuous tension and strain. Inasmuch as he was a man who suffered with a depression and an interpretation of his own predicament through depressive eyes the matter of his recovery or non-recovery was discussed, even including self-destruction. He, at all times, denied any preoccupation with such thoughts and even though his construction of the future possibilities as they affected him were nebulous he not only agreed but frequently volunteered that he was certain that he would be able to reach a level of adjustment which would bring him greater happiness, especially through more intimate contacts with his family from whom he had felt somewhat separated because of the pressure of work and also because of the opportunities for less hurried and constructive endeavors which his new freedom would permit. He was actively interested in sports and had participated in them to a considerable extent when he was younger, following the various sporting events, not deeply but enough to be fully informed about them. He was interested in history, especially, and enjoyed discussions that pertained to historical backgrounds of various situations from the time of Alexander the Great on up to the present and often wove a very interesting course into the fabric of his conversation pertaining to these historical and philosophical backgrounds and would draw comparisons and analogies with more recent happenings. To cover the rather intimate conversations which occurred almost daily for six weeks would run the gamut of all interesting subjects that a man of his erudition and background could bring into a conversation. I was more often the listener than the speaker. He did some reading but acknowledged that he found it rather trying and tiresome to attempt reading material of any profundity. He was a man of simple tastes so that repeated inquiries as to things which might make him comfortable or more contented or happier in his present hospitalization were usually met with the response that he deeply appreciated our efforts to be helpful and rather than offer a direct rejection he would usually say "Well, perhaps I will try it a little later." He frequently commented on the pleasant relations he had with all the people here and was unstinting in his praise of the personnel, the physical properties of the hospital and everything pertaining to it. My observations of his reactions during the period indicated would be that of a man who was experiencing a depressive episode which even in itself, in the absence of organic findings, would be self-limited. He was well preserved physically for his years, having a very youthful way of handling himself in all spheres and he was a very acute person intellectually. He was a man of unfailing graciousness in his reaction to even small favors and in spite of a rather austere exterior he was quite accessible for the discussion of his problems and it was very easy to feel the warmth of his friendliness in any discussions with him. Therapeutically, perhaps, I should indicate that the first week he was rather heavily sedated and this was followed by a period of treatment by sub-shock insulin. At night he did receive sedation. At first this was mandatory but he accepted it without protest and later it was made more optional as he seemed to improve and there were occasions when he expressed the opinion that he felt he could sleep quite well without sedation and would do so. If this was not the case he would be given a medication a little later. He had very few visitors because of the nature of his illness and the restraints which were imposed on visiting for therapeutic reasons. He accepted these limitations without protest and, in fact, was not particularly anxious to have visitors until he himself felt in a better mood for seeing them. Physically, his condition seemed to improve, manifested partly by his gain in weight which, although not remarkable, was at least a thrust in a favorable direction. I believe he gained about five pounds from the time of his admission but this replaced only a portion of about twenty pounds which he had lost previously. Supplementary feedings were included to hasten the recovery of his lost weight. At no time did I ever hear him express any uncertainly that he would not recover nor did I ever hear him express any threat to destroy himself. In regard to the evaluation of the trend of his condition it was indicated by his externalization and ability to express confidence in his return to health that his condition could be considered as showing the usual type of improvement expected in this type of illness. There is an unevenness about the recovery from depressed situations so that there were times when he was less animated than at other times but the depth of the depression, as measured by his responsiveness to external stimuli of all types clearly indicated that he was following the course which is seen in depressions which are lifting or recovering. In keeping with what is considered to be intelligent psychiatric measures his privileges were extended in accordance with what seemed to be his ability to handle them. It has been consistently the endeavor of enlightened attitudes in the treatment of mental illness to offer them all necessary encouragement to believe they will again be able to identify themselves with society. Perpetual isolation on a very restricted level could have a very deleterious result even in a self-limited type of depression but we considered that a patient undergoing this type of emotional distress is already the victim of overwhelming feelings of social inadequacy, inferiority and dejection. The converse of that would be the utilization of any measures which would help to persuade him that this was not true. Entirely in keeping with such an interpretation of the therapeutic needs of the patient suffering from this type of illness Mister Forrestal's privileges were extended. This had been instituted, I believe, by as much as three weeks before his death and he handled those privileges very well conforming entirely to the limitations and yet to a considerable extent embracing the enlarged opportunities for socialization. I saw nothing in his behavior nor did I detect anything in his conversations at any time which would have made it consistent to reverse the therapeutic endeavor. Inasmuch as the illness is characterized to a considerable extent by self-deprecating interpretations and because of the moral quality of Mister Forrestal's make-up it would be very difficult for him to lie and he was confronted at relatively frequent intervals with a full evaluation of the potentials of his illness so that even had we failed to be acutely conscious of over-extending his privileges it is my opinion that he would have constricted them of his own volition. If I were to offer an opinion regarding his ultimate act I would construe it as a very impulsive gesture which could not have been predicted by any means which he revealed either in his conversations or his actions. I would base this opinion not only on my own observation but my discussion with the people who were with him prior to the time of his impulsive act.

Examined by the board:

5. Q. Doctor, were you in agreement with the general principles of therapy and their mode of application in this case?
   A. Yes, sir.

6. Q. Captain, I believe you stated that there had been no attempts at self-destruction to your knowledge by the patient in question while a patient at this hospital?
   A. Yes, sir.

7. Q. Even though there had been such attempts is it still consistent with good psychiatric practice to withdraw restrictions as the patient progressed in recovery?
   A. Yes, indeed, sir.

-32-

ALL B6

8. Q. What is your opinion in placing a patient with suicidal tendencies above the ground where he may be in a position to fall or to jump from such position?

A. Your question would invite a long dissertation on all potentials of suicide. I have seen patients who hang themselves from door knobs and found it necessary to hold their knees up from the floor while they were doing it. I have known of an instance where a patient cut her throat while the nurse was sitting by her bed reading to her so that self-destruction is a force that is so impelling that it is beyond the ability of the normal mind to comprehend its depth and intensity. The desire to die under those circumstances as I have witnessed it is only comparable to the desire of a normal, healthy person to live and if you could reverse the situations wherein a healthy, normal man is threatened with life extinction and reverse that to the point where you could conceive of a man desiring to die exercising the same force and intensity of purpose it will, in a small way, measure the power behind a suicidal gesture. So far as being above the ground floor is concerned, in many hospitals they keep their most disturbed and suicidal patients on the top floor whether it be ten, fifteen or thirty stories above the ground but in all decency and respect for the prospects of the patient with a self-destruction illness they erect certain safeguards which are assumed to be adequate. Those measures were taken with Mister Forrestal when they were positively indicated but the release of the stringency of those mechanical and physical forces were lessened as he improved. This consisted mostly of giving him a little greater movement about the floor but not much beyond that.

Neither the recorder nor the members of the board desired further to examine this witness.

The board informed the witness that he was privileged to make any further statement covering anything relating to the subject matter of the investigation which he thought should be a matter of record in connection therewith, which had not been fully brought out by the previous questioning.

The witness said that he had nothing further to state.
The witness was duly warned and withdrew.
The board then, at 4:30 p.m., adjourned until 9:00 a.m., tomorrow, May 25, 1949.

THIRD DAY

NATIONAL NAVAL MEDICAL CENTER
BETHESDA, MARYLAND.

WEDNESDAY, MAY 25, 1949.

The board met at 9:10 a.m.

Present:
Captain   Medical Corps, U. S. Navy (Ret.) Active,
Senior Member;
Captain   , Medical Corps, U. S. Navy,
Captain   , Medical Corps, U. S. Navy,
Commander   Medical Corps, U. S. Navy, and
Lieutenant Commander   Medical Corps, U. S. Navy, members;
and
Lieutenant   , Medical Service Corps, U. S. Navy, recorder.
Mrs.   Civilian, reporter.

-33-

The record of proceedings of the second day of the trial was read and approved.

No witnesses not otherwise connected with the investigation were present.

A witness was called, entered, was duly sworn, and was informed of the subject matter of the investigation.

Examined by the recorder:

1. Q. State your name, rate and present station.
   A. _____ hospitalman second, U. S. Navy. I am attached to the Naval Medical School Blood Chemistry Department.

2. Q. What were your duties on the night of May 21, 1949?
   A. I was on laboratory watch that night.

3. Q. Would you please tell the board all you know about what happened on the night of May twenty-first in relation to the death of the late Mister Forrestal?
   A. I was sitting in the watch room reading a magazine that night when I heard a loud crash which came like across the passageway which is the Department of Bacteriology. My first thoughts were that a large stove or oven in that room had fell down to the floor. I ran in to investigate what the noise was, looked around the laboratory, didn't see anything wrong; don't know what prompted me, just happened to look out the window overlooking the ledge and saw something white laying out there; couldn't see very well, opened window and looked out and saw a man's body lying there. Immediately I ran back to the watch room, woke up other man on watch, he was sleeping. I called the Information Desk reported I found a man's body and to come up to the passageway opposite three seventy-three. I ran back into bacteriology. I climbed out the window, felt the man's wrist to see if there was any pulse beating; I didn't feel any. This other man on watch came. I told him to wake up the Chief who was on watch and notify him what happened. When I was out on the ledge I heard the stretcher coming up from the main floor. I ran out, I was running all the time, and showed them where the body was and there was a doctor and some attendants. The doctor climbed out the window and made his examination and that's all I had to do with it.

Examined by the board:

4. Q. What time was that?
   A. The time that I called the Information desk was zero one-fifty. That was the exact time which I called the Information Desk. There were two windows; the window from which I first discovered the body was unscreened. It kept falling down. When I went to climb out the window I used the opposite window and pushed out the screen that way. I was there most of the time the doctor was examining him and can say that the body was not moved in any way.

5. Q. To your knowledge, were you the first one to see the body?
   A. So far as I know, sir, yes, sir I was. When I called the Information Desk they acted like I was the first one who called them, they didn't seem to know anything about it previous to my calling.

-34-

6. Q. Would you please describe in detail the condition of the body as you first saw it?
   A. It was a little dark, couldn't see very well, but could see that there _____ much below the right ___; right leg seemed to be straight out in a natural position, left ___ laying over it and extending one to two feet below the right leg. I could see that he had _____ and that's all. He was laying face down. At the time I didn't notice the bathrobe; I couldn't see that well to notice it. Remember seeing something there but didn't know it was a bathrobe cord or was around the man's neck. First I knew was when the doctor came up and he had a flashlight and shined the light on the man's head; that's the first I saw of the bathrobe cord. When the doctor shone the light you could see one end was tied around his neck and other end extended over toward the left part of his head. It was not broken in any way and didn't seem to be tied on to anything. I looked to see whether he had tried to hang himself and see whether a piece of cord had broken off. It was all in one piece except it was tied around his neck. I noticed his watch; didn't notice whether it was working or not but didn't think to see whether it was running or not; didn't think about it at the time. His left arm was extended out to the side and that's how I tried to take his pulse.

7. Q. Do you know the name of the doctor who appeared on the scene?
   A. The first doctor who appeared on the scene was Doctor _____ I believe he was the junior Officer-of-the-Day that night. The doctor didn't bring a flashlight. It was brought up, I believe, by a corpsman after the doctor arrived. I am not sure of that. I was outside on the ledge and didn't see what was going on inside.

8. Q. Can you tell us anything more about the articles of clothing which were on the body?
   A. All I noted that was on the body was pajama tops and bottoms; didn't notice anything particular about them. I went down to the morgue when the body was brought to the morgue. The laboratory watch doubles as morgue watch after ten o'clock and I was down in the morgue when they brought the body in. Doctor _____ cut off his pajamas. There was no bagroom watch and so I wrapped the pajamas in a sheet and laid them aside with a tag on them marked "Please Save". Doctor _____ cut the cord off while cutting off his pajamas and as far as I know he took that with him.

9. Q. Was this bathrobe cord tight or loose about his neck?
   A. Couldn't tell you exactly how tight it was but Doctor _____, before he cut it off, he tried to insert his fingers in between the man's neck; don't know how loose it was.

10. Q. How long did you stay at the scene?
    A. I was at the scene from the time I discovered it until after the doctor came there and stayed there awhile after the doctor was there except for the time when I ran out to tell the stretcher bearers where to come; they were turning down the opposite end of the passageway. I heard the elevator and ran out. That is the only time I left the body after finding it.

-35-

11. Q. How long was the body on the roof before it was moved to the morgue?
    A. I'm not sure of that time; I believe it was somewhere between four and four-thirty. They were waiting for photographers and also Admirals   and   and it was after they gave permission that the body was moved.

12. Q. What was the approximate time? Would you say one or two hours?
    A. I believe - I couldn't say for certain, but I believe it would be about two hours or two and a half hours. The body was logged in the morgue. I logged it in the morgue.

Neither the recorder nor the members of the board desired further to examine this witness.

The board informed the witness that he was privileged to make any further statement covering anything relating to the subject matter of the investigation which he thought should be matter of record in connection therewith, which had not been fully brought out by the previous questioning.

The witness said that he had nothing further to state.

The witness was duly warned and withdrew.

A witness was called, entered, was duly sworn, and was informed of the subject matter of the investigation.

Examined by the recorder:

1. Q. State your name, rank and present station.
   A.   Lieutenant junior grade, Medical Service Corps, U. S. Navy, U. S. Naval Hospital, National Naval Medical Center, Bethesda, Maryland.

2. Q. What were your duties on the night of May twenty-first?
   A. Maintenance Watch Officer.

3. Q. During the time that you were on duty did you have occasion to see the body of the late James V. Forrestal?
   A. I did.

4. Q. Under what circumstances?
   A. It was laying on the projection roof of the third deck opposite room three eighty-four.

5. Q. Did you also have occasion to see that body after it was removed from the deck?
   A. I did.

6. Q. Where was that?
   A. In the morgue.

7. Q. At that time did you have occasion to see anyone remove a bathrobe cord from the body?
   A. I did.

8. Q. What happened to that cord after it was removed from the body?
   A. I kept it in my custody, locked it in the Officer-of-the-Day's safe and turned it over to Lieutenant   on Monday morning.

-36-

9. Q. I show you a cord; can you identify it?
   A. That is the cord.

10. Q. Is it in the same condition which you received it?
    A. It is.

The bathrobe cord taken from the body of the deceased was presented to the board as an exhibit. There being no objection, it was so received. A description of the cord is appended marked Exhibit 4.

Examined by the board:

11. Q. Could you tell the degree of tightness of this cord around Mister Forrestal's neck?
    A. It was taut, Captain, sir.

12. Q. Who gave you the cord?
    A. I wouldn't say for sure, Captain, I think Doctor   but I don't know; either he or one of the morgue attendants; they were on the opposite side from where I was standing.

Neither the recorder nor the members of the board desired further to examine this witness.

The board informed the witness that he was privileged to make any further statement covering anything relating to the subject matter of the investigation which he thought should be a matter of record in connection therewith, which had not been fully brought out by the previous questioning.

The witness said that he had nothing further to state.

The witness was duly warned and withdrew.

A witness was called, entered, was duly sworn and was informed of the subject matter of the investigation.

Examined by the recorder:

1. Q. State your name, rank and present duty station.
   A.   , hospitalman chief, U. S. Navy, Naval Medical School.

2. Q. What were your duties on the night of May twenty-first?
   A. I had the Master-at-arms duty, Naval Medical School.

3. Q. Would you please tell the board all you know relative to the events which took place on the night of May twenty-first in regards to the death of the late James V. Forrestal?
   A. I was awakened about two o'clock by   and he said that Mister Forrestal had died and I got up and went out to where he was and the Officer-of-the-Day of Medical School and Officer-of-the-Day of the Hospital was there. Everything seemed to be under control and about an hour later I went back to bed.

4. Q. What did you see and what did you do?
   A. I saw the body lying there and I didn't do anything.

-37-

ALL B6

5. Q. Where was the body?
   A. It was laying on the ledge just outside the Bacteriology Media room.

Neither the recorder nor the members of the board desired further to examine this witness.

The board informed the witness that he was privileged to make any further statement covering anything relating to the subject matter of the investigation which he thought should be a matter of record in connection therewith, which had not been fully brought out by the previous questioning.

The witness said that he had nothing further to state.

The witness was duly warned and withdrew.

The court then, at 11:55 a.m., took a recess until 1:15 p.m., at which time it reconvened.

Present: All the members, the recorder, and the reporter.

No witnesses not otherwise connected with the investigation were present.

The testimony of the following two witnesses was taken out of chronological sequence because one of the witnesses was required to be absent at a later date.

A witness was called, entered, was duly sworn, and was informed of the subject matter of the investigation.

Examined by the recorder:

1. Q. State your name, rank and present station.
   A. _____ Rear Admiral, Medical Corps, U. S. Navy; Medical Officer in Command, U. S. Naval Hospital, Bethesda, Maryland.

2. Q. Admiral _____ as Commanding Officer of the U. S. Naval Hospital what was your connection with the handling of Mister Forrestal's case?
   A. I was aware that he was going to be admitted on April second of this year, the afternoon of the second of April.

3. Q. At that time, Admiral, did you leave?
   A. No, sir, I was detached Sunday, April third, and left here at three p.m., checked out with the Officer-of-the-Day the morning of April third.

4. Q. What time did you return?
   A. I returned Friday, April fifteenth.

5. Q. At that time would you tell the board your connection with Mister Forrestal's case, if any?
   A. Well, I was in constant contact. Captain _____ the Medical Officer in charge, kept me daily informed about his progress and his condition and on numerous occasions, on two occasions, I was up with the Defense Secretary, Mister _____ for a visit and also with President _____ when he was out to visit with him and I daily was on the floor but not in the room with Mister Forrestal.

-38-

Examined by the board:

6. Q. What are your feelings in regard to the type of handling and treatment Mister Forrestal received during the period after your return and resuming command of the hospital?
   A. I feel that Mister Forrestal had nothing but the best of care; that I have all the confidence in the world in the psychiatric staff of this hospital and I feel that the statement that Captain _____ has made publicly is what he believes and I believe that Mister Forrestal had as good care as he would have received in any institution.

Neither the recorder nor the members of the board desired further to examine this witness.

The board informed the witness that he was privileged to make any further statement covering anything relating to the subject matter of the investigation which he thought should be a matter of record in connection therewith, which had not been fully brought out by the previous questioning.

The witness said that he had nothing further to state.

The witness was duly warned and withdrew.

A witness was called, entered, was duly sworn, and was informed of the subject matter of the investigation.

Examined by the recorder:

1. Q. State your name, rank and present station of duty.
   A. _____, Captain, Medical Corps, U. S. Navy, Executive Officer, U. S. Naval Hospital, National Naval Medical Center, Bethesda, Maryland.

2. Q. Captain _____ would you state what your specific duties were between the periods of April third and April fifteenth?
   A. During the period April third to fifteenth I was acting Commanding Officer of the U. S. Naval Hospital, Bethesda, Maryland.

3. Q. As the Commanding Officer during that period what was your connection with the handling of Mister Forrestal's case?
   A. As Commanding Officer during that period my connection with the handling of Mister Forrestal's case was as outlined in the Manual of the Medical Department for Commanding Officer's responsibilities on all cases in the hospital.

Examined by the board:

4. Q. What are your feelings in regard to the method of the handling and care in Mister Forrestal's case?
   A. Mister Forrestal had been placed under the direct charge of the Chief of the Neuropsychiatric service of the Naval Hospital and placed in a room on the sixteenth floor of the main building which had been secured by screening all windows and the placing of a special twenty-four hour watch on his case. In addition, a medical officer was assigned to be present during the evening hours on the same floor and sleeping in the adjoining room to the patient. All known precautions were exercised and competent personnel were constantly in touch with him. I was fully satisfied during the period that everything was being done for the welfare and protection of the case.

Neither the recorder nor the members of the board desired further to examine this witness.

The witness said that he had nothing further to state.

The witness was duly warned and withdrew.

A witness was called, entered, was duly sworn, and was informed of the subject matter of the investigation.

1. Q. State your name, rank and present station.
   A. _____, Lieutenant junior grade, Medical Corps Reserve, U. S. Naval Reserve, National Naval Medical Center, Bethesda, Maryland.

2. Q. Doctor _____, what were your specific duties on the night of May twenty-first?
   A. I was the intern on watch at the Admission Desk.

3. Q. Would you please tell the board the events relative to the death of the late James V. Forrestal?
   A. At the time that Mister Forrestal fell I was making a phone call on some other business concerning another admission that came in that night and the Chief of the Day came into the admission room quite agitated and said that somebody had fallen out of the tower and would I come immediately? I gave the phone to someone else and went with him and we took a stretcher up to the third floor to the room just inside where he had fallen. I was called at twelve minutes of two and we arrived there at about five minutes of two, the delay being accounted for by a mistake in direction. We didn't go to the right room at first and when I got there I saw Mister Forrestal's condition and checked his vital signs and they were absent, and noted his _____ which, at that time seemed incompatible with life and I pronounced him dead at that time. The Officer-of-the-Day was called at that time and I immediately had a bed-check made of the tower and his absence, that is Mister Forrestal's absence, was noted. The Officer-of-the-Day, Doctor _____, arrived at two o'clock and noted Mister Forrestal's condition and he and Doctor _____ was the other intern on watch at that time at the Admission Desk went to perform the duties of notification and Doctor _____ ordered me to stay by the body until further notification. I did so. The Navy photographers arrived at three fifteen and finished their work at three twenty-five and then when Admirals _____ and _____ arrived, don't know exactly what time it was, after they had seen Mister Forrestal Admiral _____ ordered me to have the body moved down to the morgue which Doctor _____ and I did together using one of the Admission Desk stretchers, at which time the coroner saw the body and made his examination and Mister Forrestal was placed in the morgue. I believe I was through at that time.

Examined by the board:

4. Q. Did you identify the body as that of Mister Forrestal or do you know how and who identified the body as that of Mister Forrestal?
   A. I didn't identify the body as that of Mister Forrestal until he was in the morgue when I think that I could recognize him, not from ever having seen him before but from the pictures in the newspapers. I don't know who made the definite identification of the body. The only other identification was that his room was empty we found out from the bed-check immediately at two o'clock that morning or there-abouts.

Examined by the recorder:

5. Q. Did you remove any of the clothing or anything attached to Mister

-40-

...orrestal's body?
A. ...s, there was.

7. Q. ...at?
A. ... watch and the sash to his bathrobe was tied tightly around his
   ...ck.

8. Q. ...d you remove that sash?
A. No, I didn't.

9. Q. Do you know who did remove it?
A. No, sir, I don't. It was done in the morgue in my presence but I
   don't remember who the person was who did it.

10. Q. ...d the coroner instruct one of the persons present to remove the
    ...ash?
A. ...s, sir, he instructed them how to remove it.

11. Q. ...at did he tell them?
A. ...e told them to cut opposite the knot, the back part, in order to
   preserve the integrity of the knot.

12. Q. Doctor, did you test how tight that sash was?
A. Yes, I did. I could insert one finger between the sash and neck
   without any difficulty.

13. Q. You don't think, then, it was tight enough to prevent the patient
    from breathing?
A. No, sir, it wasn't.

14. Q. Can you give the exact time that you pronounced Mister Forrestal
    dead?
A. Exact time to within a minute, sir; one fifty-five.

15. Q. ... the time that you called tower sixteen were they aware that
    Mister Forrestal was absent?
A. ... didn't call tower sixteen; I ordered it done by one of the
   ...psmen; ordered them to telephone each ward in the tower and make
   an immediate bed-check; I didn't do it myself, sir, because I felt
   that my presence was more required at the man's side because at that
   time we were not sure that he was beyond repair.

16. Q. On your examination of the body did you note any evidence of
    strangulation or asphyxia?
A. No, sir.

Neither the recorder nor the members of the board desired further to
examine this witness.

The board informed the witness that he was privileged to make any further
statement covering anything relating to the subject matter of the investigation which he thought should be a matter of record in connection therewith, which had not been fully brought out by the previous questioning.

The witness said that he had nothing further to state.

The witness was duly warned and withdrew.

-41-

A witness was called, entered, was duly sworn, and was informed of the subject matter of the investigation.

Examined by the recorder:

1. Q. State your name, rank and present station.
   A. _____ - _____ Lieutenant Commander, Medical Corps, U. S. Navy, Assistant Radiologist, U. S. Naval Hospital, National Naval Medical Center, Bethesda, Maryland.

2. Q. What were your specific duties on the night of May twenty-first?
   A. Medical Officer-of-the-Day, U. S. Naval Hospital, Bethesda, Maryland.

3. Q. Will you please tell the board the events of the night of May twenty-first in relation to the death of Mister Forrestal?
   A. At approximately zero one fifty-five I was awakened and called to the third deck, to room three eighty-four and there outside of the north window I saw a body, apparently dead. By that time the intern acting as assistant Officer-of-the-Day had arrived at the scene and had pronounced the body dead as of zero one fifty-five. A systematic search of all floors on the tower was instigated and the information was received that the room of Mister James Forrestal was empty and that he couldn't be found on the sixteenth deck. Immediately following this, Admiral _____ Commanding Officer of the hospital was notified of the death and the tentative identification of the body as that of Mister Forrestal. The Commanding Officer wished to make the notification to higher authorities of the Navy Department and therefore no notification was made by the Officer-of-the-Day's office. A guard consisting of the civilian guard, the Chief Master-at-arms and laboratory corpsman was placed in the vicinity of room three eighty-four to see that the body and general scene was not changed or molested. Admiral _____ and Admiral _____ came to the hospital within a matter of fifteen or twenty minutes and took over further arrangements. At approximately three thirty-five this officer was asked to contact Doctor _____, the Montgomery County Coroner. The coroner arrived at approximately zero four fifteen. While talking to the coroner he gave his verbal permission over the phone to move the body if we so desired before his arrival at the hospital.

Neither the recorder nor the members of the board desired further to examine this witness.

The board informed the witness that he was privileged to make any further statement covering anything relating to the subject matter of the investigation which he thought should be a matter of record in connection therewith, which had not been fully brought out by the previous questioning.

The witness made the following statement:

It might be noted that the immediate discovery of the body was within a matter of seconds by two laboratory corpsmen including _____ hospitalman second, who determined that the body was dead, went for a stretcher, notified the Chief Master-at-arms, the assistant Officer-of-the-Day and Officer-of-the-Day in rapid sequence.

-42-

Neither the recorder nor the members of the board desired further to examine this witness.

The witness said that he had nothing further to state.

The witness was duly warned and withdrew.

A witness was called, entered, was duly sworn, and was informed of the subject matter of the investigation.

Examined by the recorder:

1. Q. State your name, rate and present station.
   A. _____, junior, hospital apprentice, U. S. Navy, Naval Medical Center, Bethesda, Maryland.

2. Q. _____, what were your specific duties on the night of May twenty-first?
   A. My specific duties were to take care of Mister Forrestal.

3. Q. What time did you go on duty?
   A. I went on duty at eleven forty-five p.m.

4. Q. Whom did you relieve?
   A. _____ hospital corpsman.

5. Q. Would you tell the board what happened from the time you took over the watch at eleven forty-five until the time that you discovered Mister Forrestal was missing?
   A. When I took over the watch at eleven forty-five _____ whom I relieved told me that Mister Forrestal was still up in his room and that he had been walking around; that he had been reading. Since I didn't know Mister Forrestal personally, (I had been on the night before, and when he woke up the next morning I didn't get to talk to him very much, I didn't know him personally), he introduced me to him and he was very friendly and said "Hello" to me.

6. Q. How many times did you speak to Mister Forrestal between the time you took over the watch and the time he was missing?
   A. Approximately three or four times.

7. Q. Did you notice anything unusual about Mister Forrestal's behavior during that time?
   A. No, sir, I didn't.

8. Q. Did he say anything to you that would lead you to believe he was in any way disturbed?
   A. No, sir, he didn't.

9. Q. At what time did you last see Mister Forrestal?
   A. It was one forty-five, sir.

10. Q. Where was he then?
    A. He was in his bed, apparently sleeping.

11. Q. Where were you at that time?
    A. I was in the room when I saw him.

12. Q. Did you leave the room at that time?
    A. Yes, sir, I did.

-43-

All B6

13. Q. Where did you go?
    A. I went out to the nurse's desk to write in the chart, Mister Forrestal's chart.

14. Q. At what time did you become aware of the fact that Mister Forrestal was missing?
    A. At approximately one-fifty a.m.

15. Q. Had you previously spoken to the doctor regarding Mister Forrestal?
    A. Yes, sir, I had.

16. Q. At what time was that?
    A. That was just before one forty-five before I went back into his room to check to see what he was doing, to see if he was asleep or resting.

17. Q. And then you left the room and went out to the nurse's desk?
    A. To write in the chart, yes, sir.

18. Q. What did you do when you discovered Mister Forrestal was missing?
    A. When I went back into the room after I had finished writing in the chart, I went over to my chair where he had been sitting while I was in his room before and since it is dark in his room, very dark, my eyes had to become accustomed to the light before I could see anything. There is a chair sitting directly in front of the night light and it is very hard to see anything at all when you first walk into the room so I went over and started to sit down in the chair; just got down in the chair; by that time I could see enough to see that he wasn't in his bed. The first thought that came to my mind was maybe he had gotten up and gone into the head and at the same moment the corpsman on duty,   , came to the door and told me I had a phone call out at the desk. I told him Mister Forrestal was gone. I went out to the desk and answered the phone call. It was   , the night Master-at-arms of the Neuropsychiatric service.   asked me if Mister Forrestal was alright. I said I didn't know, that he wasn't in his bed and he told me to make a thorough check and find out for sure where he was. So I went back into the room and the corpsman gave me a flashlight and I went into the head, looked in the closet, any possible place in the room, and on my way back out in the hall back to the phone I looked into the galley and I didn't see him in there, either. So I went back to the phone and told   that he was not there.

Examined by the board:

19. Q. Just prior to discovering that Mister Forrestal was missing did you hear any unusual noises coming from the vicinity of the diet kitchen?
    A. No, sir, I heard nothing.

20. Q. Were you close enough to the diet kitchen to hear if there had been any unusual noises?
    A. Yes, sir, I definitely would have.

21. Q. What is your regular assignment in the hospital?
    A. I was on night duty on ward 6-D, a neuropsychiatric ward.

22. Q. How long have you been there?
    A. Approximately two months, a little over two months, sir.

23. Q. How long have you been assigned to the neuropsychiatric service?
    A. A little over two months, sir.

-44-

ALL B6

24. Q. How many times did you say you stood watch on Mister Forrestal?
    A. Part of Friday night and I took the regular watch on Saturday night.

25. Q. Did Mister Forrestal do very much wandering about his room or corridor Saturday night?
    A. He was walking around his room and he did follow me out to the diet kitchen when he asked me for some orange juice and then once after that he was out of his room to drink a cup of coffee.

26. Q. Did he go in the diet kitchen for the coffee?
    A. Yes, sir, he did.

27. Q. Were you with him then?
    A. No, sir, I was not.

28. Q. He served the coffee himself?
    A. No, sir, the corpsman on duty,   , was bringing coffee up in a coffee pot at that time. I was out writing my chart and he went past my desk where I was sitting and entering in the chart. He went out towards the galley with this pot of coffee and I heard him mention Mister Forrestal's name and say something to him and ask him if he would like a cup of coffee. Mister Forrestal said "Yes" and then I heard a noise which would signify he was giving him a cup of coffee and right after that I got up and went out to the diet kitchen. He was coming out with this coffee in his hand. He handed me the cup of coffee and said he was all finished with it. He said I could put it in the galley.

29. Q. About what time was that?
    A. That is one time I don't remember.

30. Q. How was he dressed?
    A. He was in his pajamas, sir.

31. Q. Did he have a bathrobe on or not?
    A. No, sir.

32. Q. Did you give Mister Forrestal any medication at all that night?
    A. No, sir, I didn't.

33. Q. Did he talk to you very much that night?
    A. No, he didn't.

34. Q. Didn't he ask you about yourself and where you come from and so on?
    A. No, sir, he didn't say much except when I first came in and was introduced to him. That was when he said "Hello" to me. When I asked him if he wanted his sleeping tablets he told me no, he thought he could sleep without them.

35. Q. Was your station inside Mister Forrestal's room or was it outside the door?
    A. I don't exactly understand what you mean by that, sir.

36. Q. Were you directed to sit in his room while you had the watch most of the time or could you sit at the nurse's desk?
    A. I was supposed to be in the room except when I went out to make entries in his chart or get something for Mister Forrestal.

37. Q. Were the lights on in Mister Forrestal's room when you took over the watch - the overhead lights?
    A. No, sir, not the overhead lights; just the night light.

-45-

38. Q. Did you notice a broken ashtray any time during your tour of duty in Mister Forrestal's room?
    A. No, sir, I didn't.

39. Q. When you were at the nurse's desk is it possible for a person to go into the diet kitchen without your observing him?
    A. I couldn't have seen him.

40. Q. Did Mister Forrestal appear cheerful or depressed in the time that you observed him?
    A. He appeared neither, sir.

41. Q. Did Mister Forrestal do any reading?
    A. Not while I was on watch, sir.

42. Q. After you discovered Mister Forrestal was gone did you go into the galley?
    A. About fifteen or twenty minutes afterwards, yes, sir.

43. Q. Would you describe the condition of the window in the area at the time that you went in there, in particular whether the screen was locked or unlocked?
    A. The screen was unlocked at that time, sir.

44. Q. Were there any attachments to the radiator?
    A. I saw none if there were.

45. Q. Did you notice any marks on the window sill?
    A. Sir, at that time I was in such a state that I didn't notice any marks on the window sill.

46. Q. You did state earlier that you had looked into the galley but no one was there?
    A. Yes, sir.

47. Q. You had no reason to examine the galley further?
    A. No, sir, I didn't.

48. Q. Did you see Mister Forrestal's body at any time later?
    A. Yes, sir, I did, in the morgue.

49. Q. Did you recognize the body as that of Mister Forrestal?
    A. Yes, sir.

Neither the recorder nor the members of the board desired further to examine this witness.

The board informed the witness that he was privileged to make any further statement covering anything relating to the subject matter of the investigation which he thought should be a matter of record in connection therewith, which had not been fully brought out by the previous questioning.

The witness said that he had nothing further to state.

The witness was duly warned and withdrew.

A witness was called, entered, was duly sworn and was informed of the subject matter of the investigation.

-46-

Examined by the recorder:

1. Q. State your name, rate and present station.
   A. _____, hospital apprentice, _____ U. S. Naval Hospital, National Naval Medical Center, Bethesda, Maryland.

2. Q. What are your regular duties at the Naval Hospital?
   A. Taking care of neuropsychiatric patients.

3. Q. How long have you been taking care of neuropsychiatric patients?
   A. Fifteen months, sir.

4. Q. What were your specific duties on the night of May twenty-first?
   A. I had the watch on Mister Forrestal from four until twelve o'clock midnight.

5. Q. During the time that you had the watch on Mister Forrestal did you notice anything unusual about his behavior?
   A. Yes, sir.

6. Q. Will you tell the board what this unusual behavior was during your watch?
   A. Well, sir, at twenty-one ten he started walking the room and it didn't seem odd at twenty-one ten but when he was still walking the floor at twenty-two hundred that was the first time he had ever walked the floor that long and he was walking the floor for a period of two hours and fifty minutes before I went off watch at twenty-four hundred. And another thing was he went into the doctors' room adjoining his room and he raised the blinds, I would say that was - don't know exact time - around twenty hundred and he raised the blinds and raised the window and at the time I was at the desk. We had orders we could stay at the desk until twenty-one hundred so long as we checked on him; so I went back to the doctors' room and the patient was standing at the window. He had raised the bottom part of it up as far as it would go. When I walked in the room he jumped aside. He had the blind to the top and the window up as far as it would go. I walked in the room and he jumped aside. He said "____, I raised that window. If it gets you in any trouble close it" so he went back through the head and closed the door so I let the blind down and walked out of the room. Just as I got to the door I heard the door to the head open again. He stuck his head out so I went back and closed the head door and locked it and I went back to the desk. I didn't make any note of it because he has opened windows several times in his own room and the doctors' room. Only difference was I am usually there with him when he does it. Other than that there was nothing odd that he done that I can think of.

7. Q. How long had you stood watch on Mister Forrestal previous to this particular night?
   A. Well, sir, I took over the watch the third day he was up there.

8. Q. Do you know what date that was?
   A. I would say it was the fifth of April.

9. Q. And you had stood watches continuously on him since that date?
   A. Yes, sir, I had eight in the morning to four in the afternoon, then I went from there to twelve to eight, stood that for two weeks, then went on four to twelve. I have been on four to twelve for a little over three weeks.

-47-

Examined by the board:

10. Q. These occurrences that you have just related in regard to Mister Forrestal's behavior on that night, did you consider them sufficiently unusual to report them to the doctor?
    A. No, sir, I reported his walking the room to Doctor ____ and I put it in the chart and then Doctor ____ asked me how come the door was locked back there and I told him I thought I better lock it being as he raised the blind.

11. Q. Did you attach any particular significance to this type of behavior?
    A. No, sir, I didn't at that time.

12. Q. Had you seen him in the past do things similar?
    A. Well, sir, he several times did walk the room. He hated light and walked over to the window shades and if they were open a little too far he would pull it closed.

13. Q. Did Mister Forrestal seem friendly on that night?
    A. Yes, sir, he seemed very friendly. I introduced ____ to him as I left the watch and he shook hands with ____ and said he was glad to meet him.

14. Q. Did he meet him the night before?
    A. No, sir, he was sleeping when ____ came on watch and hadn't awakened by the time ____ went off.

15. Q. Other than the conversation you have given with Mister Forrestal did he say anything else to you on that night?
    A. No, sir, he asked me if I thought it was stuffy in the room and he asked that several times since I have been on watch; he liked fresh air. When I was on night watch, twelve to eight in the morning he always got a blanket out for us to wrap around us because he had the windows wide open.

Neither the recorder nor the members of the board desired further to examine this witness.

The board informed the witness that he was privileged to make any further statement covering anything relating to the subject matter of the investigation which he thought should be a matter of record in connection therewith, which had not been fully brought out by the previous questioning.

The witness made the following statement:

He started reading a book at about twenty hundred and whenever the corpsman would come in the room he would turn the bed lamp off and sit down in the chair and so far as the writing I don't know. It appeared that he was but I couldn't say for sure.

Neither the recorder nor the members of the board desired further to examine this witness.

The witness said that he had nothing further to state.

The witness was duly warned and withdrew.

A witness was called, entered, was duly sworn, and was informed of the subject matter of the investigation.

Examined by the recorder:

1. Q. State your name, rank and present station of duty.
   A.   Lieutenant, Nurse Corps, U. S. Navy, presently stationed U. S. Naval Hospital, Bethesda, Maryland.

2. Q. What are your regular duties at the Naval Hospital?
   A. At the present time I am on night duty from ten until seven covering from tower eight to tower seventeen, inclusive, supervising all wards.

3. Q. What were your duties the night of May twenty-first?
   A. I was on night duty from ten until seven, covering towers twelve to seventeen, inclusive.

4. Q. Will you please tell the board the events relating to the death of Mister Forrestal on the night of May twenty-first?
   A. Yes. I had started rounds, gotten my reports on fourteen, was through there about twenty after ten; made rounds on fourteen, went to thirteen then fifteen and I reached sixteen shortly after eleven. At that time I went in to see Mister Forrestal. He wasn't in his room. He was out in the galley having orange juice with the corpsman,   I spoke to him then and he was very calm and self-assured and quite pleasant. He returned to his room. Then, I think about eleven thirty, I went down to tower ten to relieve the nurse on duty there. It is a dependents' floor and military female floor. After relieving her I went to supper, returned to tower sixteen I would say approximately one o'clock. I checked on Mister Forrestal then. My corpsman had just found him in the galley and the lights had been out when the corpsman,   , went in. Mister Forrestal came toward him. He had some coffee with him for the night. Mister Forrestal asked about having some coffee and was quite friendly with the corpsman. Mister Forrestal left the galley and returned immediately to his room.   the corpsman on Mister Forrestal at that time was charting at the nurse's desk. I told   that I wanted to be informed if Mister Forrestal didn't sleep as I was aware of the fact that he had pretended to take his sodium amytal earlier in the evening but it was found he hadn't, that he had been quite active. I understood that   before being relieved of his watch at midnight had discussed Mister Forrestal with Doctor   who was on duty. Mister Forrestal, after drinking his coffee, went to bed. I made short rounds and came back and checked on Mister Forrestal again, went into the room. This was at one thirty and he was in bed at that time and I assumed him to be sleeping. I asked   if he thought he was asleep and   thought so. Within seconds after I left the room   came out and told me as soon as I walked out of the room Mister Forrestal asked who that was who had entered the room. The room was in total darkness with the exception of the very small night light which was partially covered by a chair; the light was dim. I sent in to awaken Doctor   and to ask him what he advised about sedation since Mister Forrestal had already refused sedation. The next thing I knew about it it was about a quarter to two when Miss   I was in the office at that time on sixteen doing the night log, when she came up and told me a body had fallen. She had heard

-49-

the sound of the body falling and I ran for Mister Forrestal's room, flipped the light on and he wasn't there nor he wasn't in the bathroom.   , the floor corpsman had run over to the galley and flipped the light on there and as you entered in the galley you could see the window open and the screen was ajar. I went in and awakened Doctor   . at that time and told him Mister Forrestal was not in his room and the galley window was open.

5. Q. Earlier in the evening when you sent the corpsman,   , in to inform Doctor   that Mister Forrestal had not taken his sleeping medicine what, particularly happened as a result of this?
   A. Doctor   told the corpsman if Mister Forrestal wanted to take his sodium amytal he could but not to force it.

6. Q. How long have you been on this particular night detail?
   A. At that time I had been on approximately a week.

7. Q. Was it usual for Mister Forrestal sometimes not to take his regular sedation at night?
   A. Not usual, but there were nights when he hadn't taken it; he hadn't taken it the night before and slept well; refused it the night before and slept well.

8. Q. When he refused to take it was it a refusal to take medicine or just a desire not to take it because he thought he probably could sleep?
   A. He thought that he would be able to sleep without it although the corpsman, when   had given it to him earlier he thought he had taken it and because of his pacing up and down he thought he hadn't taken it and questioned him and he told him he hadn't taken them.

9. Q. Had you known of that to take place at any previous time, that is, that he pretended to have taken his capsule and didn't?
   A. Not since I have been on night duty but it seems to me while I was on day duty there that that had happened, cannot remember the particular day.

10. Q. On one occasion?
    A. Yes, I seem to remember it having happened before; he didn't like to take sedation but usually took it.

11. Q. On that particular night in question did you notice that he appeared unusual in any way or more agitated, more disturbed, more distraught than usual?
    A. At the time I saw him in the galley close to eleven thirty he appeared his usual self; very cheerful, pleasant but no different than at any time I had ever seen him.

12. Q. So far as you know was it usual for Mister Forrestal to go into the diet kitchen on the floor?
    A. I wouldn't say I thought it was usual. I knew he was having increased activity during the day but not at night.

Neither the recorder nor the members of the board desired further to examine this witness.

The board informed the witness that she was privileged to make any further statement covering anything relating to the subject matter of the investigation which she thought should be a matter of record in connection therewith which had not been fully brought out by the previous questioning.

The witness made the following statement:

I think I should say my reason for being so particularly interested in Mister Forrestal that night was I didn't like the fact he had been so active earlier in the evening and he hadn't taken his sodium amytal. I understood from the chart when I came on that he had more or less increased motor activity. He had been quite active and I just thought I, perhaps, should pay a little more attention to him since I knew there was a new corpsman on and I would prefer him remaining in bed than having him move around as freely as he was doing.

Neither the recorder nor the members of the board desired further to examine this witness.

The witness said that she had nothing further to state.

The witness was duly warned and withdrew.

A witness was called, entered, was duly sworn, and was informed of the subject matter of the investigation.

Examined by the recorder:

1. Q. State your name, rate and present station.
   A. _____, hospital apprentice, U. S. Navy, Bethesda Naval Hospital.

2. Q. What are your regular duties?
   A. Right now I am on night duty. Every hour I make my rounds on my regular patients on tower sixteen.

3. Q. On the night of May twenty-first what were your duties?
   A. As usual I made rounds every hour and at twelve o'clock I was relieved to go to chow.

4. Q. Were you the regular night duty corpsman on tower sixteen?
   A. Yes, sir.

5. Q. Will you tell the board the events leading up to the time of Mister Forrestal's death on the night of May twenty-first?
   A. As much as I had seen him. I believe it was around nine thirty the regular special watch came out and ordered a half-glass of orange juice which I got. He went back in his room and drank it and I never seen him; thought I heard him stirring, talking to the special watch. I went to chow and came back up. We go down about one o'clock and get some fresh coffee. I went down and come back up and just as I went in the galley, I thought the door was all the way open which it wasn't, I found out when I bumped into the door with the coffee. I pushed it open and seen him and he come towards me, patted me on the back real cheery like and I asked him if he wanted a cup of coffee which he took and went in his room. Then I heard the special watch bring the empty cup back out and sit it in the galley and that's the last thing I knew. I never seen the man no more.

-51-

6. Q. And you had any particular dealings with Mister Forrestal previously?
   A. No, sir, only when he first come and during the day I was on day work then and detailed certain rooms to clean. That room was my room to clean but we never touched it. The vacuum cleaner and all come up from downstairs, never went in there. Only time I seen him was when we went in the head to swab and that stopped and I never did see him after that. That's the only other dealings I had with the man.

7. Q. When did you first become aware of the fact that Mister Forrestal was missing?
   A. I got a telephone call from the Information Desk to hold a bed-check which I did. I was getting ready to go back to check his room, had checked other patients and the phone rang again and they wanted his special watch to come to the phone so I went there and told him he had a phone call. I got the call approximately one forty-eight; never looked at the clock. When he got the call he come to the phone, went back and he said he wasn't in there. He said sometimes he used to, when he got lonely, there were two beds in the opposite room, in the doctors' room, sometimes he would go over and lay down with him. So I gave the boy my regular flashlight I always carry and said go into the head and see if he is there; he come back and said he wasn't. By that time the nurse come and turned the light on and I went out and turned the galley light on and I seen the screen was loose. That's all I know.

8. Q. Did you see Mister Forrestal on any other occasion on the night in question - on any other occasion than running into him in the diet kitchen?
   A. Only nine-thirty when he asked for that glass of orange juice.

9. Q. How did he seem at that time?
   A. He seemed very cheerful to me like he did at one o'clock. At one o'clock he patted me on the back, don't remember just what he said, sounded real cheerful to me. I asked him if he wished a cup of coffee and he said Yes he would like to. He asked me if I was going to have one and I said "Yes" and he poured one out for me, picked his cup up and went back in the room.

Examined by the board:

10. Q. Was Mister Forrestal alone in the galley at the time you brought the coffee up?
    A. Yes, sir.

11. Q. Where was the special watch at that time?
    A. That was at one o'clock. He was just logging something in his chart, heard me talking to Mister Forrestal and he came right out there.

Neither the recorder nor the members of the board desired further to examine this witness.

The board informed the witness that he was privileged to make any further statement covering anything relating to the subject matter of the investigation which he thought should be a matter of record in connection therewith, which had not been fully brought out by the previous questioning.

The witness said that he had nothing further to state.

The witness was duly warned and withdrew.

A witness was called, entered, was duly sworn and was informed of the subject matter of the investigation.

Examined by the recorder:

1. Q. State your name, rank and present station.
   A. _____, Lieutenant junior grade, U. S. Naval Reserve, U. S. Naval Hospital, Bethesda, Maryland.

2. Q. What are your regular duties at the Naval Hospital?
   A. I am on night duty from eight to twelve just about two nights a week, Thursday and Friday. For some time I was scheduled for the month but the civilian nurse on one twenty-eight got sick and I am over there and Miss _____, the relief nurse for the civilian nurse, relieves on one twenty-eight on Thursday and Friday and I take the lower towers eight to twelve.

3. Q. What were your particular duties on the night of May twenty-first?
   A. Usually before quarter of two I go down to tower eight before I write the Captain's log and I had left tower twelve and went down to tower eight and I asked the corpsman how everything was and he said he just gave a man a pill. I happened to look up at the clock. It was just about one fourty-four. I sat there in a chair for a minute and then I heard this noise. It was a double thud and I said what was that. I said "It sounded like somebody fell out of bed you better check the wing in front" and he went to check the beds and said it was alright so I said "I'll check the head" and sent him to tower seven to see if it was something down there. That's when I walked in the bathroom on tower eight. I looked out the window. I just remember thinking in my mind, "Oh, my God, I hope he isn't mine" and I ran up to tower twelve and told the corpsman to check on Colonel _____ room so he walked into his room and I walked into room twelve thirty opposite his room and looked out the window from there and could see a body distinctly. It was then I really realized it was a body and I thought of Mister Forrestal. So I went up to tower sixteen and told Miss _____ there was a man's body outside the galley window and he wasn't mine. We both went into his room and he wasn't there and we noticed the broken glass on the bed and looked down and noticed the razor blade and told him he was missing and she said it was one forty-eight. Then I walked over towards the galley and noticed the screen was unlocked. That's about all.

Examined by the board:

4. Q. When you found out the body was not that of one of your patients what made you think of Mister Forrestal?
   A. I knew he wasn't mine and I knew that Mister Forrestal was up there and was being watched.

5. Q. You said you saw his slippers and a razor blade beside them; where did you see them?
   A. The bed clothes were turned back and towards the middle of the bed and I looked down and they were right there as you get out of bed.

-53-

...ographs that I shall pass over to you. These are photographs of the external injuries, taken just before the time of autopsy. We took two photos, one of the skull and one of the abdomen. I have copies of these and also have the negatives which, if the board wishes, I could turn over.

Examined by the recorder:

5. Q. Captain _____ were there pictures taken of the autopsy of the late James V. Forrestal?
   A. There were pictures taken of the external injuries immediately preceding the autopsy.

6. Q. Captain, I show you two pictures, can you identify them?
   A. Yes, these are copies of the pictures that were taken of which I have just spoken.

The two photographs were submitted to the board by the recorder and offered as evidence. There being no objection they were so received and are appended marked Exhibits 5A and 5B.

Examined by the board:

7. Q. Doctor, did the brain show any pathological findings beside those of trauma?
   A. There were no other pathological findings except those due to the acute trauma.

8. Q. Is there any evidence of strangulation or asphyxia by strangulation?
   A. No, there was absolutely no evidence external or internal of any strangulation or asphyxia.

9. Q. Were there any slashes across the wrists?
   A. There was a laceration of the volar surface of the right wrist which was a part of the general lacerations due to the recent fall. This wrist,

   wrist. However, there was no evidence of any lacerations that would in any way appear to have been self-inflicted either recent or remote.

10. Q. Was there any fracture of the cervical vertebrae as shown by X-Ray of the body?
    A. The X-Ray didn't reveal any fractures of the cervical vertebrae; that is the X-Ray taken prior to autopsy didn't reveal any fractures of the cervicle vertebrae.

Neither the recorder nor the members of the board desired further to examine this witness.

The board informed the witness that he was privileged to make any further statement covering anything relating to the subject matter of the investigation which he thought should be a matter of record in connection therewith, which had not been fully brought out by the previous questioning.

The witness made the following statement:

The cause of death appearing evident I have no further statements to make.

-55-

Neither the recorder nor the members of the board desired further to examine this witness.

The witness said that he had nothing further to state.

The witness was duly warned and withdrew.

The board then, at 4:03 p.m., adjourned until 1:15 p.m., tomorrow, May 26, 1949.

FOURTH DAY

NATIONAL NAVAL MEDICAL CENTER
BETHESDA, MARYLAND.

THURSDAY, MAY 26, 1949.

The board met at 1:15 p.m.

Present:

Captain   , Medical Corps, U. S. Navy (Ret.) Active,
Senior member;
Captain   , Medical Corps, U. S. Navy,
Captain   Medical Corps, U. S. Navy,
Commander   Medical Corps, U. S. Navy, and
Lieutenant Commander   Medical Corps, U. S. Navy, members;
and
Lieutenant   Medical Service Corps, U. S. Navy, recorder.
Mrs.   Civilian, reporter.

The record of proceedings of the third day of the investigation was read and approved.

No witnesses not otherwise connected with the investigation were present.

A witness was, at his own request, recalled to introduce some additional evidence which he had at hand and was warned that the oath previously taken by him was still binding.

Examined by the recorder:

1. Q. State your name, rank and present station.
   A.   Captain, Medical Corps, U. S. Navy, U. S. Naval Hospital, National Naval Medical Center, Bethesda, Maryland, Chief of the Neuropsychiatric Service.

Examined by the board:

2. Q. Doctor   did you request to reappear before the board to submit some further statement and letters into the testimony?
   A. I did, sir, inasmuch as Doctor   was the original psychiatrist in Mister Forrestal's case I thought the board should know of a letter which I have just received from him, dated May 25, 1949, and headed the American Psychiatric Association in Annual Meeting at Montreal, Canada. It is signed by Doctor   as President of the American Psychiatric Association.

-56-

3. Q. Do you recognize the signature?
   A. I do. I know Doctor _____ signature quite well and this is it without a question of a doubt.

4. Q. Will you proceed to read the letter to the board?
   A. The body of the letter which is addressed to me is as follows:
   "Dear Doctor _____ I was very sorry to learn of Mister Forrestal's death. As you know, I have been familiar with the total situation from the beginning and have kept in close contact with what was being done. I fully approved of the treatment outlined for him. As a physician, I know it requires greater medical courage to take reasonable risks in the course of recovery than to retain restrictions which retard the getting-well process. If there is anything I can do to help the public or otherparties concerned to understand the unpredictable nature of a person with an extreme, impulsive drive to self-destruction, please let me know." I have also a number of other letters if you are interested in any of them. They have been streaming in.

Doctor _____ letter was presented to the board by the recorder and offered _____ evidence. There being no objection it was so received and a photostatic copy is appended marked Exhibit 6.

5. Q. If you have some other letters you think would be worthwhile to submit to the board we would be glad to hear them.
   A. If the board is interested, here is a letter from Doctor _____, Professor of Psychiatry, University of Michigan and consulting psychiatrist to Selective Service during the recent war. It is addressed to me and signed by Doctor _____ whose signature I know quite well; written on hotel stationery from Montreal, Canada, under date of May 25, 1949. "Dear Doctor _____ I have read the newspaper accounts of the tragic death of Mister Forrestal and I am writing to express my sympathy to the family, physicians and to the United States Navy for the loss of such a vigorous former leader and Secretary. I am also concerned that the widespread publicity might in some way reflect upon the excellence of Navy psychiatry unless there is full understanding by everyone of the necessary risks and hazards which must be faced courageously in the management of such a medical problem. Modern psychiatric treatment requires that certain planned risks must be undertaken on occasion in order to facilitate recovery and rehabilitation. No precautions can guarantee avoidance of tragedy in a patient with powerful, impulsive self-destructive tendencies. To utilize constant surveillance precludes the return of self-confidence in the patient and may arouse irritable uncooperativeness in an individual of determined and forceful personality and thus may defeat the whole plan of therapy. It is my sincere hope that this letter may be of some slight comfort to you and that it will emphasize some of the difficult decisions which arise in the therapy and management of such cases.".

Doctor _____ letter was presented to the board by the recorder and offered evidence. There being no objection it was so received and a photostatic copy is appended marked Exhibit 7.

I would like to say that there are numerous other letters but these two I present first because Doctor _____ knew the case quite well and

-57-

second because Doctor _____ pretty well sums up the contents of all the others. There are perhaps twenty from various psychiatrists including one from Doctor _____, Superintendent of St. Elizabeth's Hospital, and from numerous other people but this, the one of Doctor _____ about summarizes what the rest of them have to say.

Examined by the board:

6. Q. Doctor, upon your return to Bethesda did you view the remains of Mister Forrestal?
   A. Yes.

7. Q. Captain _____, in reviewing the previous testimony we recall that you described a weekly cyclical pattern as part of his general trent toward recovery. Can you give us any explanation for that pattern?
   A. As nearly as I could tell the increasing depression in Mister Forrestal's case towards the end of the week was rather directly related to his fear of further attacks by certain commentators who broadcast on Sunday evening. It so happened that these two individuals had been particularly vicious in their personal attacks and he was extremely sensitive about further attacks from them. He was so sensitive about these broadcasts that he refused to listen to them himself but asked that I keep an accurate record of what they said. As he improved he was quite disturbed, and reasonably so, over one Sunday night broadcast which had alleged that he was wildly insane and distorted in his judgment while still a Member of the Cabinet. The content of that particular broadcast, which I recorded, had no basis whatsoever, in fact. Mister Forrestal found that particular broadcast an especially hard one to deal with, as he got better, because there seemed to be no way in which it could accurately be disposed of by him. The most difficult single problem in the management of the case was the wild attitude of certain sections of the press. Mister Forrestal was kept isolated from contacts as a part of his treatment. It was our belief that he needed at least two months of rather complete freedom from contact, even with his friends, to permit a good recovery. His friends and family were totally cooperative in this as they had been in all stages of treatment. Certain sections of the press, unfortunately, were not.

Neither the recorder nor the members of the board desired further to examine this witness.

The board informed the witness that he was privileged to make any further statement covering anything relating to the subject matter of the investigation which he thought should be matter of record in connection therewith, which had not been fully brought out by the previous questioning.

The witness said that he had nothing further to state.

The witness was duly warned and withdrew.

The board then, at 1:55 p.m., adjourned until 9:00 a.m., Tuesday, May 31, 1949.

FIFTH DAY

NATIONAL NAVAL MEDICAL CENTER
BETHESDA, MARYLAND.

TUESDAY, MAY 31, 1949.

The board met at 9:00 a.m.

Present:
Captain _____ Medical Corps, U. S. Navy (Ret.) Active,
  Senior member;
Captain _____ Medical Corps, U. S. Navy,
Captain _____ Medical Corps, U. S. Navy,
Commander _____ Medical Corps, U. S. Navy, and
Lieutenant Commander ____ Medical Corps, U. S. Navy, members;
and
Lieutenant _____ Medical Service Corps, U. S. Navy, recorder.
Mrs. _____ Civilian, reporter.

The record of proceedings of the fourth day of the investigation was read and approved.

No witnesses not otherwise connected with the investigation were present.

Captain _____ Medical Corps, U. S. Navy, was recalled as a witness and was warned that the oath previously taken by him was still binding.

Examined by the board:

1. Q. Captain _____, you have stated that from mid-May the next thirty days were considered to be the most dangerous in the convalescence of Mister Forrestal. Why did you go to Canada during this critical period?

   A. The stage of therapy had reached the point where it was necessary for the patient to develop some independence from the therapist. It had been developing rather steadily from about the tenth or eleventh of May. I fix the date at that because it was just prior to Mrs. Forrestal's departure. This was a normal movement in therapy and one which eventually had to be accomplished to make therapy successful. As I have stated before, Mister Forrestal was very close to recovery and actually I felt that this was the last hump that he had to get over. That is one reason for considering it such a dangerous period. The patient has to undergo a developing independence of his therapist and it is in that period of resumption of his own independent personality that stresses are sometimes too great for a patient. Had I not left town I would have spaced my interviews out to accomplish essentially the same thing. I called the hospital on Thursday night and talked to Doctor _____. One reason for the call was to be sure that Mister Forrestal had reacted to my departure as had been expected. I had intended calling on Sunday morning for a further check on his condition.

-59-

2. Q. Captain _____, do you mean that this period of risk was created by the break in close dependence upon the therapist and not by other factors in the chronological course of recovery?
   A. No, I think I said that is one of the reasons it is a danger period. The two are not clearly separated; don't know how to separate all of the factors involved. That is to say, it is chronological and yet is also a function of the therapy; they go hand in hand and I don't know quite how to separate them in any more clear fashion - they go together.

3. Q. Captain _____, do you consider that your continued duty at the Naval Hospital would have in any way altered the course of Mister Forrestal's acts?
   A. No, sir.

4. Q. It is noted in Doctor _____ letter that he refers to the "unpredictable nature of a person with an extreme, impulsive drive to self-destruction." To clarify this statement the board would like to know if you consider this impulsive drive would be a constant factor or one of momentary urge?
   A. I felt in Mister Forrestal's case that the drive which led to his actual suicide was a momentary urge and the grave danger that existed throughout was that we could never have enough security to protect against such a flash of depression; for example, had the entire floor been screened, the fire exits offer an opportunity for suicide, or had he wished, he slept in a darkened room, he could easily have cut his wrist and the corpsman would never notice it until the next morning probably, if it were done under the covers. There were so many suicidal opportunities that could not be removed under any circumstances that this type of impulse was extremely difficult to deal with. There was nothing in his previous history or behavior to indicate that there would be such an impulsive move, but the possibility of it was recognized.

5. Q. Did Mister Forrestal listen to the radio?
   A. Yes.

6. Q. Did Mister Forrestal listen to the broadcasts of the commentators that you previously mentioned?
   A. No.

7. Q. Was this information as given by the commentators transmitted to Mister Forrestal by you and if so, to what degree?
   A. He had access to it through the newspapers and he and I discussed what he had read but I can't say how much I transmitted to him. He had free access to incoming mail, newspapers, books and there was a great deal of comment about one of the broadcasts which occurred after Mister Forrestal's admission to the hospital. The comment was editorial and in various syndicated columns.

Neither the recorder nor the members of the board desired fruther to examine this witness.

The board informed the witness that he was privileged to make any further statement covering anything relating to the subject matter of the investigation which he thought should be a matter of record in connection therewith, which had not been fully brought out by the previous questioning.

The witness said that he had nothing further to state.

The witness was duly warned and withdrew.

The investigation was finished, all parties thereto withdrawing.

After full and mature deliberation, the board finds as follows:

FINDING OF FACTS.

1. That the body found on the ledge outside of room three eighty-four of building one of the National Naval Medical Center at one-fifty a.m. and pronounced dead at one fifty-five a.m., Sunday, May 22, 1949, was identified as that of the late James V. Forrestal, a patient on the Neuropsychiatric Service of the U. S. Naval Hospital, National Naval Medical Center, Bethesda, Maryland.

2. That the late James V. Forrestal died on or about May 22, 1949, at the National Naval Medical Center, Bethesda, Maryland, as a result of injuries, multiple, extreme, received incident to a fall from a high point in the tower, building one, National Naval Medical Center, Bethesda, Maryland.

3. That the behavior of the deceased during the period of his stay in the hospital preceding his death was indicative of a mental depression.

4. That the treatment and precautions in the conduct of the case were in agreement with accepted psychiatric practice and commensurate with the evident status of the patient at all times.

5. That the death was not caused in any manner by the intent, fault, negligence or inefficiency of any person or persons in the naval service or connected therewith.

Captain _____, Medical Corps,
U. S. Navy (Ret.) Active, Senior member.

Captain _____, Medical Corps,
U. S. Navy, member.

Captain _____, Medical Corps,
U. S. Navy, member.

Commander _____, Medical Corps,
U. S. Navy, member.

Lieutenant Commander _____,
Medical Corps, U. S. Navy, member.

Lieutenant _____, Medical Service
Corps, U. S. Navy, recorder.

-61-

NATIONAL NAVAL MEDICAL CENTER
BETHESDA, MARYLAND
OFFICE OF THE MEDICAL OFFICER IN COMMAND

June 1, 1949

A review of the evidence in the foregoing investigation into the facts and circumstances leading up to the death of the late Mr. James V. Forrestal reveals:

That the deceased was admitted as a patient to the U. S. Naval Hospital, Bethesda, Maryland, on April 2, 1949. That at the time of his admission to the hospital his condition was what was described by the medical officer in charge of his case, and who is a qualified psychiatrist of some eighteen years of experience in that specialty, as "obviously quite severely depressed" and "exhausted, physically".

Because of his mental and physical condition, an immediate twenty-four hour a day watch consisting of constant surveillance was established over the patient, adequate orders for the patient's safety were issued, and a regime of medicinal therapeutics commenced; the latter to alleviate his depressed condition and to build up his physical strength. The patient's response to the treatment was considered to be good, though of a gradual and irregular nature.

During the period of the deceased's hospitalization, the psychiatrist in charge of his case, Captain C   . MC, U. S. Navy, talked with him concerning the question of self destruction. It was fully realized by Captain   and his chief assistant, Captain   MC, U. S. Naval Reserve, a qualified psychiatrist of some twenty-nine years of experience in his specialty, that the deceased considered suicide at times and that a patient with that type of disability is a potential suicide. In view of this knowledge on the part of these two medical officers, adequate instructions were issued to personnel assigned to the constant attendance of the patient as to measures to be carried out to safeguard him.

The record further shows that on April 26, 1949, the restrictive regulations in force in the deceased's case were eased but that it was discovered that his condition had not improved to the extent to justify such action; therefore, on April 29th an order was issued to the attendants on watch to the effect that they must stay in the room with the patient at all times, for as late as that date it was considered that the patient still entertained suicidal tendencies at times. However, the patient's condition showed an abrupt change for the better and on May 1st, because of this improvement, the close surveillance was relaxed during the afternoon watch. About May 5th the close watch was further relaxed, the patient's door was allowed to be left open, on May 7th the day watch was relaxed to the extent that the watch was not required to remain in the patient's room at all times. The patient's condition continued to show further improvement to the extent that it was not necessary to administer sedatives each night to provide relaxation and sleep. Toward the middle of May the patient's condition had improved to the extent that it was considered that "He was very close to well, actually" and that only about thirty days more of hospitalization would be required. About May 18th, due to the improvement in his case, he was encouraged to see and talk with people and to extend his activities. At this time it was considered that the patient had progressed to the point where a well calculated risk of suicide was advisable to be taken as a part of his treatment, to prevent the fixing of a permanent mental stigma in and irreparable damage to the patient's mind and to aid him in making a complete recovery. The patient was allowed to use the telephone and to make other contacts, within a clearly defined sphere of operation.